Smarter Property Improvement

Smarter Property Improvement

Ways to maximise returns by transforming your property

PETER CEREXHE

ALLEN&UNWIN

First published in 2004

Allen & Unwin
83 Alexander Street
Crows Nest NSW 2065
Australia
Phone: (61 2) 8425 0100
Fax: (61 2) 9906 2218
Email: info@allenandunwin.com
Web: www.allenandunwin.com

National Library of Australia
Cataloguing-in-Publication entry:

Cerexhe, Peter.
Smarter property improvement: ways to maximise returns by transforming your property.

Includes index.
ISBN 1 74114 060 9.

1. Real estate investment – Australia. 2. Real estate development – Australia. I. Title.

332.63240994

Typeset in 10.5/13 pt Slimbach by Midland Typesetters, Maryborough, Vic.
Printed by Southwood Press Pty Ltd, Sydney

10 9 8 7 6 5 4 3 2 1

Contents

Acknowledgments and disclaimer ix
Introduction: Squeezing blood from stone xi

Section I Improving your investment

1 **Why me? Why *not* me!** 3
Succeeding as an active property investor • 'everyone's doing it . . . so should we' • sharing the load • 'we made money . . . but it tore us apart' • more than one way: exploring your options • property development syndicates

2 **Strata apartment solutions** 19
Strata development strategies • old units, new views • yesterday's kitchen • space for the car • inside the roof • strategies for negotiating with the body corporate • necessary maintenance—a hindrance or an opportunity to improve? • sizing up an apartment block

3 **Developing a house** 37
One 'L' of a house • catching the 'lame ducks' • strategies for renovation • house trends which present opportunities for development • expanding the floorspace, shrinking the footprint • overcapitalisation: know your market • lifting the *whole* property to a new level

• marketing strategies which drive renovation • a safety plan • the business of creating solutions • gain 100 per cent more garden and 30 per cent more home • measure the return in terms of additional rent • ten rules of renovation • sizing up a house for redevelopment

4 **Medium-density housing** 67
Building in the backyard • going further: multiple townhouses • beginner's luck . . . or smart planning? • medium-density guidelines • what does the surveyor do? • sizing up a site for medium-density development

5 **Changing the permitted use** 79
'Change of use' strategies • a hook to hang your hat on • principles for pursuing a 'change of use' application • sizing up a property for a change of permitted use

6 **Subdivision: drawing new lines on the land** 88
Pros and cons of land subdivision • roads and building envelopes • subdivision checklist • get an expert guide • filling in the details • legal encumbrances • working in unfamiliar territory • shape and access options • playing by the numbers • sizing up a subdivision site

Section II Working with your experts and the council

7 **Seeking council approval** 111
Know the terminology • handling objections • who gets notified? • defence tactics: making your own objection • defensive strategies • the written objection • getting consent • hired gun: the town planning consultant • strategies for using a town planning consultant • a less compromised perspective • dealing with council officers • designing your way into trouble

8 **Working with your designer** 130
What does an architect do for you? • should I use an architect or a designer? • what it will cost • where things can go wrong • 'It's just what I asked for! I'm so unhappy!' • mistakes with measurements

• the design brief • getting things round the right way • check the details • cross-cultural problem-solving

9 **Working with the builder** 145

• Making a contract • who regulates or licenses builders? • how to handle contractual variations • delays • finding a remedy

Section III Money and risk

10 **What will it cost me?** 157

Development costs • illustration of project costs • stamp duty on transfer • stamp duty on mortgages • tax: get in tune with it • Capital Gains Tax • will you be paying too much tax? • ABN and GST • financing the project • using the comparison rate for different loans • why use a registered valuer?

11 **Getting out of trouble** 178

Back-up strategies • swap shop • a bet each way

12 **A final word: Motivation** 186

The screwer gets screwed • too close to your property? • the one that got away

Resources, information and contacts 193

Land titles offices • industry associations • architects • surveyors • consulting engineers • registered property valuers • finance • tenancy information • law societies • industry complaints handling schemes • property reports and marketing • your finances • credit • taxation • consumer protection agencies and associations • builder licensing authorities and associations

Glossary 205

Index 217

Acknowledgments and disclaimer

When it comes to matters of precise detail, including tables, I would like to acknowledge specifically the personal assistance and resources of the Australian Taxation Office, the Australian Bureau of Statistics, state and territory revenue offices and builder registration/licensing authorities, together with Warwick Horsfall of Habitat Planning, Geoff Stean of Stean Nicholls and the Real Estate Institute of Australia, without which this book would not have been possible. I acknowledge the input of individuals, materials and websites of the state/territory fair trading offices and building industry organisations (including the RAIA, Archicentre, HIA and MBA). My heartfelt thanks go to the subjects and sources of the various case studies and other anecdotes, and Katie.

I consider it unfair to talk about people and their money and then potentially identify them or their projects. Out of concern for their privacy, I have changed the names of all involved and particulars which might reveal the actual development projects. The lessons are the most important aspects of the case studies.

The subject matter of this book traverses a huge range of facts, figures and opinion. Government regulation and industry practice are changing constantly, and in important ways. While accuracy has been an important part of the preparation for this book, readers must seek up-to-date information and expert personal advice before acting or refraining from acting on anything contained herein. In particular, you are encouraged to discuss your plans with a licensed financial planner, accountant and solicitor; the author is not a licensed financial planner and this book is intended to provide information of a general nature only, not financial, taxation or legal advice.

Peter Cerexhe

Introduction: Squeezing blood from stone

The problem with buying a brand new strata unit as an investment is that everything's been done already—it's been optimised for current fashions, and you can't work with it to extract hidden value.

You can do better than that. Rising property prices over recent years have created an opening for investors to squeeze more value out of their property investments through developing the potential of a site.

Investors all want two layers to their cake:

- capital gain;
- yield or cashflow.

But smarter investors also want the cream in the middle:

- transformation gain.

This last kind of benefit is all the more important when property prices are high. Values have outstripped rental returns, so yields are way down. The '5 per cent yield' for residential property investment is a memory. Expenses—stamp duty, agent's commission, mortgage repayments, advertising for a tenant and ongoing running costs—are a substantial drain. Simply getting a foothold in the property market has been a major task. It will take years to return to a point where rental income approaches a more affordable proportion of holding costs.

The two-layered cake is mostly undemanding of us. It's a simple, well-used and familiar recipe for wealth creation. The ingredients are:

- **capital gain**. All the work is done by the time you exchange contracts to purchase the property. If you've chosen wisely, you have bought yourself a bargain. With time, and reasonable economic conditions, capital gain will emerge automatically. It is supremely *passive*. The economy looks after you.
- **yield**. A little negotiation—obtaining the right interest rate on your mortgage, getting the managing agent to reduce their commission, obtaining quotes on maintenance work—will improve the cashflow from the property. This isn't mere passive investing—but you don't raise a sweat either.

However, if your property is suitable for **transformation gain**, you're getting into *active* investment. Not everyone wants to do it or has the time and/or spare money to do it. But it can represent a good return on the time, effort and cash it takes to develop your property investment.

Property transformation can radically increase the payoff for the investor, above and beyond merely owning and renting out a property. Here's an illustration: a property had been owned for three years—a home on a large block of land with a hefty mortgage.

- If sold now, it would return $100 000 to the owner as gross profit from passive capital gain.
- If the owner didn't sell, but instead got plans drawn up for a couple of townhouses in the backyard and then obtained development consent from council, it could be sold as a development site for $200 000 gross profit.
- If the owner stayed on, obtained construction approval, engaged a builder and built the townhouses for sale, his or her profit would double again, to $400 000.
- Or the owner could keep one of the townhouses as his or her home and live in it mortgage-free (or substantially so) after selling off the others.

At what stage would *you* want to bail out of that property? The passive capital gain level, the development approval level or the completed project level? If your property wasn't a house, but a strata unit, would you take the necessary steps to gain approval to enclose a balcony, to convert common property to private property, to change the floorplan to maximise views and light?

This book is about **transformation gain**: how to find a property investment which offers the third layer of financial benefit and how to exploit this opportunity in practical terms. As a development lawyer for many years, I worked with people who took property and shook it into more profitable shape. These are the lessons they taught. Working with property has brought me into contact with many more ordinary investors—barbers, clerks, doctors, journalists, computer programmers—who have amazing tales to tell of their own efforts to maximise the value they obtain from property. I've used their stories to illustrate key points for property transformation. You'll find that a large part of the technical side is easy enough to sort out when you speak to council and engage your experts. For my money, however, the smarter stuff comes from seeing what creative souls have done with their properties and how they have problem-solved.

Residential property is the focus here. There's no doubt there is money to be made out of commercial and industrial redevelopment, but these are areas where the investor hazards *all*. Take a drive through a couple of local industrial areas and you can usually see factories which are unsaleable other than as demolition sites. The building fabric has had its day and refurbishment would be a waste of time and money. Similarly, local shopping centres have an economic life beyond the small investor's influence. If just one important shop tenant departs the scene, the whole centre can suffer terminal decline.

You can be clever and you can be lucky in developing commercial and industrial property. But casualty rates are high. By comparison, residential development has a surer market. If you mess up the figures, or things go wrong, you will suffer—but it is unlikely you will get into as much trouble as you would with commercial or industrial property. So residential property is a good place to start.

What's more, you are probably quite familiar already with residential property. Maybe you've bought and sold a few properties over the years. This is an excellent base camp from which to scale the next mountain.

Any ideas of development must be seen in the context of the economy, mostly here in Australia—although overseas events (September 11, the plummet in stock prices, the 'tech wreck', recession in key overseas economies) have clearly had an impact on our corner of the globe. Trends in borrowing and household spending reveal where the action is going on. Consider these patterns which have emerged in housing and finance:

- **We are borrowing more**—mostly for housing. Around 84 per cent of household debt is tied to housing (owner-occupiers and investors) compared with around 70 per cent in the early 1990s. In 1990, the average new mortgage across Australia was around $74 000. By 2003, it was sitting just under $200 000.
- **We are escalating our borrowing for investment**—over the last decade, loans for investment in residential property have increased significantly faster than for owner-occupation. The annual average growth over 1990–2002 was 21.7 per cent for investor housing, but only 13.2 per cent for owner-occupied housing. Over the same period, investor loans as a share of total household debt went up from 9 per cent to 26 per cent.
- **Housing loans are the new business**—according to the Reserve Bank, Australian banks reached the position in 2003 where they had the same lending exposure to the housing sector as they do to the business sector.
- **We are using property mortgages to buy consumables**—cars, holidays, lifestyles. More than 30 per cent of mortgaged home owners did this. Rising house prices helped fuel this trend (housing values have risen since 1990 at an annual rate of 8.75 per cent nationally and rose 17 per cent over 2001–02 alone), as did ready access to redraw facilities and line-of-credit loans secured against property.
- **We are refinancing our mortgages**—the trend to switching loans from one lender to another increased at an annual rate of 29 per cent over 2000 and 2001. Why? To obtain cash to spend on our lifestyles, to get into a loan with more favourable terms than our current deal, and to consolidate a number of loans into

one place and product. Financially, we have itchy feet—and we are always on the lookout for a slightly better deal.

- **Property prices continued to climb at the same time as vacancy rates were rising**—average tenancy vacancy rates were above 4 per cent in Sydney and Melbourne and much worse in pockets of these cities. Tenants were negotiating hard for better deals and lower rents. This shook the complacency with which many investors viewed their bulging property portfolios. Risk returned to the property party.
- **We are becoming property investors**—around 9 per cent of Australian households now own investment property. It is no longer just for the financial elite.

So, we are home owners, we are property investors, we are strongly attracted to property, we are living with an increased awareness of risk and we are restless in our finances. It is natural that many of us will take the next step and transform our property into something more valuable, keeping more of the profit for ourselves.

Section I

IMPROVING YOUR INVESTMENT

1

Why me? Why *not* me!

Succeeding as an active property investor

I can barely read financial magazines without becoming nauseous at the advertisements for riches through property investment. Like the deeply serious Slow Food movement—which advocates a retreat from meaningless fast food and a return to food prepared for taste and nourishment for the body and soul—we need a Slow Wealth movement. What those ads preach is a crash-and-burn philosophy where the winners get profiled and adored while the losers get no media attention. They just disappear out of the equation. It's a convenient fiction. And it's the financial equivalent of fast food.

Slow Wealth has the same destination as the Rush to Wealth school but simply takes longer. You've got to warm up and stretch before you sprint. So how's your attitude?

Nowhere in financial matters is attitude more important than in the realm of property transformation. The stakes are high and success is never a 'sure thing'. Greed has a place, as do ego and the thrill of doing the deals. Yet their impact is magnified when it comes to working with property. Foolishness and excessive greed are punished hard, although not always the first time around.

Importantly, you are not operating on your own (as you generally are when you buy shares or acquire passive investment property). For most of us, property transformation is a big step beyond any property dealings we've entered before. You are caught up in a zone where your financial security is linked with a host of professional consultants and with local communities. Property transformation is a rollercoaster ride. So what does it take to succeed?

- **Charisma**. This is undoubtedly the prime factor which distinguishes many of those who are actively and successfully working to reshape their property with council consent.

  I have worked with a number of such people and never ceased to be amazed at what they could get away with. One man—successful and charming—faced a financial crisis when his plans were caught up in council. 'Until I get those plans approved and released, the bank won't let me have any more money. And the builders are about to lynch me!' he said. 'I've got to get those plans out!'

  I informed him that council's best estimate was two weeks for approval and release—and that was if they decided to give his file priority. So he headed off from my office to council chambers. It was two o'clock in the afternoon and the council closed at four. Two hours was all he had.

  Sure enough, he returned to my office at 4.30. In his hand were the plans—duly stamped and signed off by the health officers, the town planning officers and several other departments. I jokingly asked him how much he had paid to get this through so fast.

  'Fifty bucks,' he replied. 'And that was for only one of the departments. All the rest expedited the plans for nothing.'

  Two hours instead of two weeks, almost entirely through charm. Amazingly, the bureaucrats *wanted* to help him out once they met him face to face. It wasn't a chore, it wasn't a duty, nor was it a legal requirement. Other people would still be sitting in the council office waiting room holding a numbered ticket from a machine.

  Council officers don't respond well to threats. To them,

you're just another property investor in trouble for having reached too far. You're trying to get rich while they are stuck with low wages. It's no good making threats. When the going gets tough, smart property investors reach down deep into their personality. If you lack charisma, you can at least be charming.

- **Self-belief**. You are going to put your ego on the line and watch while people jump up and down on it. The love of money—or, for many, the love of *making* money—is not enough to sustain most of us through the lengthy, demanding process of getting plans through council and the construction phase, particularly when neighbouring property owners lodge objections, write letters to the local newspaper and phone you at night. What keeps successful property transformers going is a strong self-belief. This is more powerful than the lure of the cash. After all, there are many other ways of making money and they will become more tempting as each hurdle is confronted.
- **Great negotiating skills**. 'You want to extend your house? Add a flat in the backyard and subdivide? Come inside, come inside! Let me lend you money; let me be your agent; let me design your building; let me sell you things!' You will be popular—everyone wants a piece of the action. It's like those movies where the hero has inherited an abandoned mine and gives a 20 per cent share to the shop owner who provides the digging tools, then a 20 per cent share to the man with the explosives; a further 20 per cent goes to the bank for financing the project; another 20 per cent is taken by the transport company; and the final 20 per cent is handed over to the government for the necessary licences and safety inspections. You're going to have to negotiate everyone down to a manageable stake in the project or you'll be left with nothing. And you will need persuasive skills to shepherd the plans through council.
- **An understanding of when the details are more important than the broad picture**. There's a lot of waffle involved in designing a project and taking it all the way to fruition. For much of the time, it's fine to talk in generalities: 'The concept is . . .'; 'We fully intend taking all necessary steps to . . .'; 'Council wants to see the best possible use of the site . . .' These rarely get you into trouble. However, the real trouble starts when

you confuse loose, conceptual chat and spruiking with absolute deadlines, mandatory requirements and precise mathematical numbers in the planning and building codes and other directives. If you don't have that high level of attention to detail, if you are not a numbers person, if your English reading or comprehension skills are not that hot, then you will need that sort of person on your team.

- **Access to even more cash in reserve than you can imagine ever needing**. Anyone can add up the costs of working with property. You find the skills and materials you need, you get the quotes, sign the 'fixed price' contracts, pay the fees—and there's the total bill. Yet it is almost a fundamental law of mathematics that the final bill will substantially exceed your budget and estimate of the cost. Here's the word which property people probably fear more than any other: delay. Every little thing which delays the project means dollars lost out of your pocket. That's why you'll need good, open access to funds.
- **Experience with property ownership**. It might seem reasonable to assume that everyone reading this book has had prior experience of property ownership, but this would be wrong. I've known people whose first experience is with inherited property—in their case, vacant land which required at least some development before it could profitably be sold off and the proceeds of the inheritance divided among the family members. Others have purchased their very first property with a view to transforming it into something more valuable or saleable. Anyone in that position should at the very least do some reading and speak to friends about what they have learnt from property ownership (including being a landlord). Learn the terminology—the people you will soon be dealing with will assume you understand the language of property and finance.
- **An understanding of marketing**. At the end of the project, you've got to sell your wares. Either you will dispose of the property/properties or you will be looking for tenants. If you have created more than one unit or residence or block of land, you will need a more thorough and thoughtful marketing plan than just delivering the property to an agent. When offloading multiple dwellings or blocks of subdivided land you need to

know what else is on the market, their pricing structures, the pros and cons of theirs and yours, how your marketing can make your property stand out, and so on. Again, this is something which can't be left just to the 'experts'.

'Everyone's doing it . . . so should we'

Bill and Julie had a comfortable middle-class life in a comfortable middle-class suburb of Sydney. Bill was a dentist who long ago had given up on private practice and moved into a government job to reduce the pressure and stress. It was still a good income. Julie had been a nurse up until the time they had their first child. For twenty years now she had been a housewife, looking after the home and the kids.

They had been in their home for so many years that it was worth quite a bundle. I had been to their home—it was Federation-ish, California bungalow-ish . . . Perhaps more 'ish' than real style. A typical big old comfortable family home on a large corner block in a good street of a good suburb.

There was a boom in apartment construction going on in the area. Several near neighbours had sold their big old homes to developers to turn into apartment blocks. A couple of neighbours had done the development themselves.

'We spoke to these neighbours,' said Julie. 'They were laughing all the way to the bank. It seemed they could *double* the value of their home just to pull it down and get some plans approved by council. They didn't even have to build the apartments themselves. They just sold the land and the approved plans to the builder. So, you see, they weren't caught up in all the stress and hassle of getting the job done and upsetting all the locals.'

Bill added: 'It seemed like anyone could do it—double their money. All you had to do was get an architect to prepare some drawings then lodge them with council for approval.

'Sure, we knew there could be problems. But there had already been two such developments approved in *our street*! There was no logical or *fair* way that our one could be opposed. In fact, it would be pointless for anyone to stand in the way. All we'd have to do was point at the two prior approvals and to others in nearby streets. They couldn't let some property owners do it and then say no to the rest, could they?'

And so Bill and Julie found themselves an architect. He was very enthusiastic about the project, noting in particular the large site and its corner location, which would assist with car access and parking in the design. It seemed a natural spot for an apartment block. In fact, said the architect, with demand for apartments at a high point there was the possibility not just of doubling their money, but *tripling* it. Everyone was excited.

So the plans were drawn up. The architect had discussions with the council officers, who seemed on side with the project. They recommended getting some other expert reports about the site and the construction so as to smooth the way through council.

The architect lodged the development plans with council and council notified the neighbours. At this point, all hell broke loose.

It seemed the neighbours had had enough. They wanted no more apartment blocks destroying their formerly quiet middle-class street. They were tired of the jackhammers and trucks which had been moving up and down from 7.00 a.m. each day for the past year. The dust, the noise, the parking problems!

For the first time in that corner of the neighbourhood, the residents got organised. They were drawing a line in the sand. Petitions were prepared and taken door to door. Hundreds of signatures were obtained protesting Bill and Julie's development.

Bill and Julie were shaking in their California bungalow/Federation home. They felt everyone's eyes on them. Even their banker had read about the growing protest in the local newspaper. Bill and Julie thought it was so unfair. 'We are always first to sign petitions and to support local issues. We're not the *baddies*!' said Julie.

A low point came when the architect told Bill and Julie that the objectors had successfully got the matter on to the agenda for the next council meeting. People could get up and say what they thought. Did Bill and Julie want to address the meeting too?

Arming themselves with righteousness, they duly made their plea to council. It was a messy night—one they would never forget. Shortly thereafter, council rejected their development application.

'Now you must go to the appeals court,' advised the architect. 'Get yourself a lawyer.'

They saw a lawyer. He told them he would be expensive. He also said he needed the assistance of a barrister. He would be more expensive. How expensive? He couldn't tell them. 'It depends on so many variables.'

And so Bill and Julie chucked in the towel. 'We were beaten,' said Bill. 'We could have pressed on—with a fair chance of winning at court. But even then the future was uncertain. And it would drain us, both financially and emotionally, to pursue the development.'

Julie made a more blunt assessment. 'It wasn't for us. We're not property developers. We aren't hungry enough. We thought we could face the challenges. Everyone around us was so positive we began to think that we were almost doing the neighbours a favour. But, fundamentally, we like to lead a quiet life. A moderate income from a low-pressure government job suits us.

'There had been a window of opportunity, if you like, for local development. But we missed it. By the time a few apartment blocks had got the green light—and started messing up the street—resentment had built and the "window" had closed. We were there at the wrong time, caught in the spotlight. Although we were "good guys", we caught the heat for those who had gone before and muddied the water.'

Sharing the load

Have you got what it takes to get development consent for your proposal? It's a mistake to think you have to be tough, unrelenting and unpleasant to succeed (though many home owners and investors are precisely that—they care for no one else, they see no one's viewpoint but their own). It is possible to succeed with integrity intact.

I believe you need the attributes listed earlier in this chapter. Importantly, however, you don't have to embody all the necessary attributes in yourself. You can find partners for the deal or you can buy the skills and toughness you might need from time to time. That's why many investors work in pairs or small teams:

- the one with the ideas and the one with the money;
- the builder and the property owner;
- the solicitor and the estate agent;
- the cashed-up doctor and the entrepreneur.

It is painfully easy for a couple, living together in a relationship, to turn property design and construction into an ordeal. It is with them, in their relationship and home, 24 hours a day for a minimum of a year or eighteen months. There is no escape. The problems and issues of the project become central to their lives.

Mess it up and you could find you've fractured your relationship as well. If you're living in the property while it undergoes transformation, you are really living dangerously.

If your investment partner is outside your domestic relationship, it gives everyone a little more space for ordinary life to proceed—which is a necessity. It inserts distance. Often it is that little extra detachment which allows business partners to know when to persist in fighting for what they want and when to call off the chase.

'We made money . . . but it tore us apart'

I had been to Francine and Rob's inner-city Victorian terrace house many times. They were in their twenties and were just excited to have their own home—a place they owned. It didn't matter much to them that most of the building was a bit of a wreck. It was comfortable enough, and all their neighbours had similar, unrenovated homes.

Time moved on, they had a couple of children, and now the limitations of the house were really making themselves felt. The crunch ultimately came when they decided they wanted to live in Europe for two or three years.

'We didn't want to sell our home but couldn't rent it out in this condition. It was OK for an owner to put up with the problems, but a tenant wouldn't take it,' said Francine.

They decided to borrow some extra money from the bank and really develop the place to its full potential. This would be much more than a makeover or refurbishment.

'The area was starting to go ahead,' said Rob. 'Property values were rising sharply and the whole suburb was becoming "yuppified". We knew we could make a good return on our investment.'

The work involved tearing down the back half of the house and rebuilding a completely new rear section. The toilet came indoors. A new bathroom, kitchen, laundry and family room were built. The entire backyard was pulled out. Off-street parking was created in the new courtyard. More stairs were added and a third bedroom was built into the roof cavity.

The household furniture was stacked up. Every surface that had not been demolished was cleaned, patched and painted. The furniture was brought back into the rooms. Then the carpets needed to be replaced—and the household furniture was stacked up once more. It was discovered that the balcony was about to fall off the front of the terrace. The upstairs furniture was moved downstairs. The balcony was made stable. The furniture was brought back up the stairs.

The family lived through it all. The two children played in the plaster dust and rubble. Francine tried to complete her university degree, writing her essays wherever she could find a flat surface. Rob came back home each day from work and found little peace or recognition for his hard day in a clean, air-conditioned office.

'The process went on for eighteen months,' said Francine. 'For the last six months we were barely talking to each other—except to complain and to pull out our hair over the mounting bills. And our European adventure? Forget it! We were on the road to divorce.'

Fortunately their stamina got them through. The house was finished, they found a tenant and headed off overseas. When they returned, some three years later, they found their home had shot up in value. And it was a home they could enjoy—although they now had a third child and were wondering about adding another bedroom. Maybe they'd sell this time . . .

More than one way: Exploring your options

You want to be an active investor but, beneath it all, you must remain in touch with financial realities. When assessing the development potential of a site, it pays to keep your investor hat on. Consider how the proposal fits in with your overall financial plan and both short- and long-term objectives.

A few years ago, Stan paid $650 000 for a good, level block of land in a central heritage location. Eight run-down, one-bedroom units sat on the block. It was always his intention to demolish the one-bedders and replace them with something more modern and valuable. The units were old—dating from the 1960s—and just hanging on to a lettable condition. The rent return was excellent: 13 per cent. It was a great holding pattern. The rent paid most of the interest and expenses of running the eight flats.

Over the next three years, Stan put little money into the units—there was no need. Rents were low, he kept the units painted and clean, and tenants were happy to have this affordable, well-located option.

But property prices have risen substantially over the past three years. Now the property is worth roughly 50 per cent more than Stan paid for it. Stan wonders if now is the right time to develop the property. 'The longer I hold on,' said Stan, 'the greater is the risk that I might have to put some serious money into maintaining the property. Things like a new roof or electrical wiring repairs or a new kitchen.'

Stan decided to discuss the matter with the managing agent for the property. It turns out there are several options to consider:

- **do nothing**: hold on to the existing flats as an investment, looking to maximise capital gain rather than income. It was a strategy that was still working;
- **fix up (Figure 1.1)**: get more rent—a 20 per cent increase in income—and continue to hold as an investment;

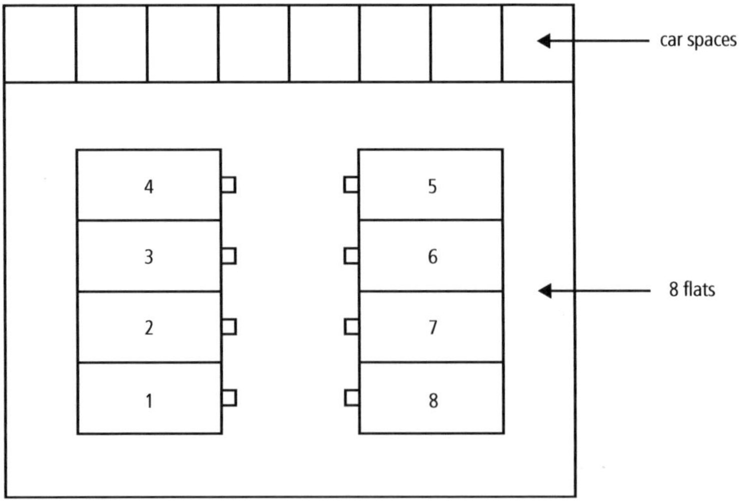

Figure 1.1: eight flats, single title

- **strata and sell (Figure 1.2)**: subdivide and sell the eight units, each with a private courtyard and parking space; this would involve minimal construction cost and net around $100 000 on sale;

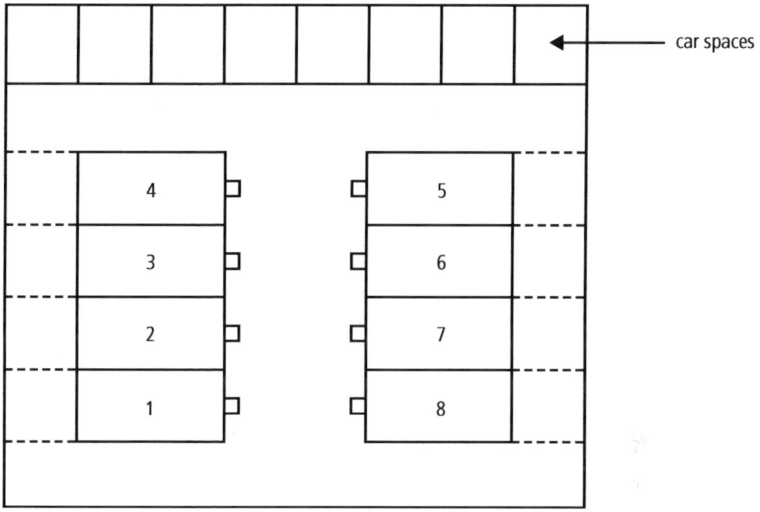

Figure 1.2: eight strata units with private courtyards—using existing structures

- **house block (Figure 1.3)**: demolish the flats and create a huge home site; this would require little effort, and maybe generate $50 000 profit on sale;

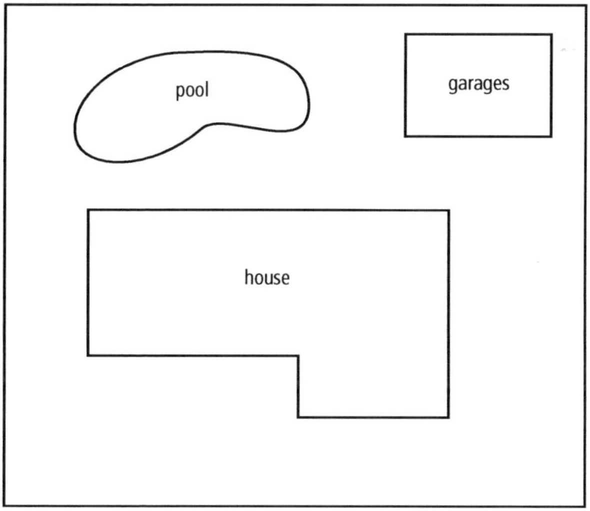

Figure 1.3: house block

- **townhouses (Figure 1.4)**: demolish the flats and construct four luxury townhouses (18 squares + garage); it would take the most effort, but would generate $600 000 on sale.

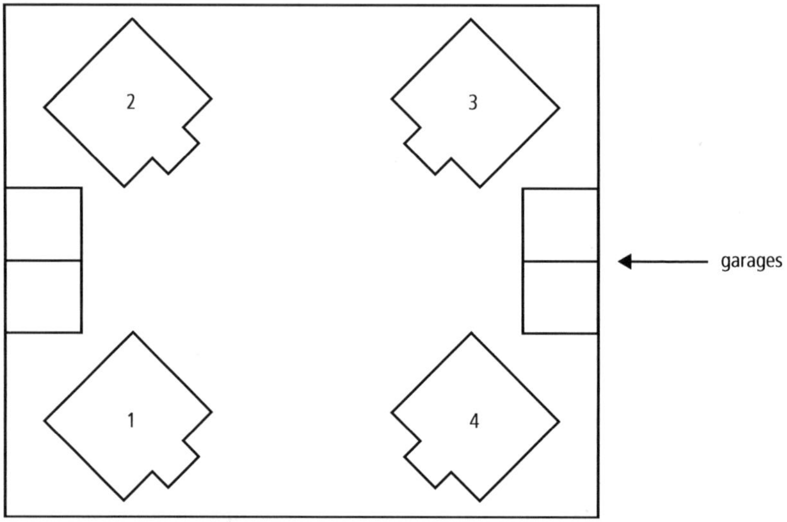

Figure 1.4: four new townhouses

Stan hasn't made up his mind yet. In this area there is a growing demand for exceptional house sites. People are quite prepared to pull down an existing house and build their million-dollar extravaganza. Stan feels that some purchasers will see the wisdom of paying considerably more for a substantial, level site in such a good location, surrounded by heritage properties. 'Neighbours will not object—they will be keen to see the old block of flats torn down and replaced with a valuable dwelling,' said Stan. 'That's a bonus to anyone wanting to build a large home.'

This is a possible option, but not a strong contender. Stan would have to persuade estate agents and purchasers to see the special value in his block. The agent—who, you remember, currently manages the units—was initially very supportive of a townhouse proposal. However, he soon realised that if the townhouses were sold off he would lose the eight flats from his rent roll. He began to back the second option: fix them up and continue to own and rent them.

But Stan was not convinced: 'Eight flats produce a great total rent, but each flat itself has a low rent. They are one-bedders—they will never justify a truly high rent. If I fix them up—painting, floor coverings, new kitchens and bathrooms—it will take twenty years for the higher rent to pay off the expense! It's not on. In a different location, with a different tenant base, it might work. But not here.'

In the end the choice comes down to the four townhouses or just hanging on to the property—undeveloped—for a few more years and enjoying the capital gain. 'If I develop the townhouse proposal myself, I stand to make around $600 000. That's a sizeable sum,' said Stan. 'But what do I then do with the money?

'I'd look around for another property to buy. Something with good capital growth potential and a sound rental return. If I am extremely fortunate, I will find a property with a 5 or 6 per cent gross return.

'But, hey, I'm getting more than that now. It will be hard to improve on what I've got already. In the end, I am sure I will go the townhouse route—that will maximise my gains when I am ready to sell. The exercise has shown me that I need to resolve what I will do with the money: will development deliver a better investment than the current property?

'Everyone wants me to develop the site—and they will all make money out of the various jobs involved. I'll sit on it a while longer—I haven't got a plan which is actually an improved situation for me.'

Most sites offer you a range of choices. Sometimes it's best to sit on it for a while and see what comes naturally. At other times it's more a matter of striking while a market segment is hot.

Property development syndicates

Property syndicates have been around for a long time, and they are popular still. In part, this is due to the rising price of property and the escalating cost of bringing services to a subdivision.

The other driver for syndicates is that so many of us lack time. We might be able to struggle through things on our own, balancing job, family, recreation and the subdivision or other development project, but at what cost? Through syndication, it is possible to share the load and split the proceeds.

You may have some friends who, like yourself, are experienced in property investment and are looking to move on to more active management of their assets. Maybe you don't know anyone who is ready and willing to join you on this adventure. If not, hunt down a smart, active real estate agent who has been in business in the relevant locality for many years. This means he or she will have built up a wide network of clients. An entrepreneurial agent will put you in touch with other potential syndicate members.

Strategies for forming property syndicates

Person A: middle aged. Has managed a number of property investments and is good with finance. Has equity sufficient to raise $300 000 towards the project. Has little time to put into it other than on weekends.

Person B: a 65-year-old woman who has just retired. From her superannuation payout she has $400 000 and is looking for a market-linked investment so that her finances don't diminish in real terms. She is willing to consider property development to boost her retirement savings. But she is not really able to put any energy into it. She will make a good silent partner.

Person C: a young, highly paid executive who is aggressively looking for opportunities. Doesn't own a home—rents near the beach at a colossal weekly cost. He wants to sell one of his cars—maybe the Porsche—and cash—in a few share options. He's got $300 000 to put into the syndicate. He works flexible hours and can handle development issues which spring up mid-week. He needs to be partnered with others who have experience with property.

Put them together and you've got a mix of abilities, ages and time to put into the project. Importantly, whereas you (person A) might have been looking at a one million dollar development, the syndicate has a million dollars in hand and can borrow probably another three. You are now contemplating a four million dollar project.

Yes, you will split the proceeds (if it turns out to be profitable).

But think how much wider your net is cast. You are no longer looking at the scraps passed over by others—the unusual block, the ugly house, the block next to the open stormwater drain. You can choose from better sites and options. You might even shift your focus from a struggling middle-class suburb to a desirable location with a more certain sales projection.

An active, entrepreneurial estate agent meets people at all stages of life who want to use the investment vehicle of property and are able to contribute in varied ways—superannuation payouts, sale of a farm, sale of a business, too much money income, medical specialists, factory owners, cashed-up retirees looking for fun, beneficiaries of deceased estates, builders.

Property syndicate contracts: The practicalities

If you enter a property development syndicate or work with a partner, you must get a solicitor to prepare a written agreement setting out the terms of the project. Discuss these issues:

- **Your contributions**. The contractual document must specify what each of you is contributing—financially or otherwise (e.g. use of existing property equity to support the mortgage; labour, cash, contacts, equity, property, time, know-how).
- **Agreed understanding**. It should say what you are expecting to happen as your *common* understanding of the project.
- **Who does what**. It should say who is responsible for each of the various tasks.
- **Who gets what**. Be clear on how the proceeds will be divided among the syndicate members.
- **Negate partnership**. It is vital that you do not inadvertently become legal partners, because partners are liable for expenses authorised by each other, even when you might not be aware of what is going on. Your solicitor can protect each of you from this potential catastrophe. You may, alternatively, wish deliberately to become partners at law. Understand the difference.
- **Timeframe**. The agreement should specify the timeframe for the project and for the syndicate.
- **Getting out early**. What happens if one of you wants to back out early? Maybe there is a divorce or serious illness which

unexpectedly darkens the horizon. Your solicitor should discuss this with you and prepare the appropriate clauses in your agreement.

- **How to bring one of the syndicate members back in line**. Two of you are working hard on the project, but the third member is coasting on your efforts—or has failed to kick in the necessary share of funds. The contract should tell everyone how to apply pressure to a non-performing member of the group.
- **Handling disputes**. How will the members resolve any conflict or disputes over interpretation of the contract or the project itself? Your contract can specify an agreed process for resolving problems. This might involve, for example, an agreed mediator.

Do it now, while everyone is happy and getting along well. Don't leave it until you are barely on speaking terms or it will cost you an arm and both legs to get out of the syndicate or to get your fair share of the profits.

Summary

- A successful active property investor possesses a number of skills and attributes, including charisma, self-belief, great negotiating skills, an understanding of when to focus on getting the details absolutely right, access to cash reserves, experience with property ownership and an understanding of marketing.
- If you don't possess all of these, you could consider teaming up with a partner who can offer them.
- Active estate agents can help link you with other investors to form a property syndicate.
- With any team, get a solicitor to put your expectations and terms into a written agreement which binds the parties.

2

Strata apartment solutions

Smarter property development is not restricted to houses and vacant land. Home units and townhouses—particularly older ones—have plenty of potential too. As they say, small fish can be very tasty.

Apartments offer a real bonus over houses when it comes to development: sometimes more than one owner is available to carry the costs. If you are a pleasant, charming person, you can use your negotiating skills to convince fellow unit holders to commit to a vision for the property. Everyone wins, so everyone kicks in a few dollars (or at least gives their necessary consent). And there are great things you can do within the confines of your own apartment—provided you have chosen astutely.

Strata development strategies

What are people doing with their units? Here are five development strategies which can be used to liberate value hidden in those anonymous piles of concrete and aluminium:

1 creating more valuable spaces;
2 finding a technological solution;
3 converting common spaces to private use;
4 improving common assets;
5 converting the legal title to a more valuable form of title.

Creating more valuable spaces

Let's see what can happen when you really think 'outside the square'.

Old units, new views

Down in a gully beside the ocean was an old block of flats dating back to the 1930s. Time weighed heavily upon them—they were in poor shape and had been too difficult and expensive to renovate. Importantly, because they had been relatively cheap (before the late-1990s/early 2000s property boom) they were now owned by people who did not have high-paying jobs—in fact, many of the owners were beach bums! They had purchased their homes here because they couldn't wait to get out of the office and on to the sand.

But now the building was worth a small fortune. The boom had finally slid into their gully and a couple of the more upwardly mobile owners wanted more from their units. Because these few worked so hard and for such long hours, they wanted to squeeze every moment of lifestyle and glamour they could from these tired, small units.

Like many old, unrenovated buildings, this block of flats had a large yard out the back. This meant they could add more room to their units without breaching council floorspace ratios and other requirements. At present, many of the units enjoyed an ocean view. Typically, this was from the main bedroom and/or the kitchen. Perhaps this had been the priority in the 1930s.

The plan was simple: add balconies to the six rear units (three storeys of two per floor across the back). These balconies could almost be bolted on to the brick wall and keyed into the floors. They could be generously proportioned, too—adding considerable value to those six units.

Of course, as the floorplan stood, the balconies would come off the main bedroom—not the best use of the new entertainment facility. With a bit of reshuffling, however, the old loungeroom could be cut off from the hallway and turned into a new main bedroom, with the existing main bedroom becoming the loungeroom. While the new loungerooms would be smaller than the old ones, the addition of the large balconies would more than make up for this.

The financial side of the development was tricky, with some owners cashed up and others hard pressed. However, those with the money carried some of the additional costs and ensured that a persuasive valuation report was provided to every owner's mortgagee.

And not only did certain unit owners get the benefit of balcony living space, the construction process allowed a number of otherwise prohibitively expensive maintenance tasks to take place on the rear wall while the scaffolding was up, enabling the whole body corporate to gain from the development.

The above example shows how it is possible to literally make money out of thin air. People miss the mark when they fail to see the special opportunities offered by apartment blocks—particularly old ones.

There are a number of other ways we can create valuable spaces in a strata unit. Note that in many cases you will need prior approval from the body corporate. Consider:

- **enclosing a balcony** to create a home office, a study, an all-weather sunroom;
- making room in the kitchen or bathroom for a washer and dryer—thus creating an **internal laundry**;
- adding split-system **air-conditioning**;
- changing the **floorplan**—depending on the construction, it might be possible to change the position of a doorway, to create a more open-space layout or to enclose a kitchen so it doesn't spill into the lounge area. To access a view, a bedroom could become a loungeroom;
- changing the **door and/or windows** leading on to the balcony to open up the view or simply to improve the space for entertainment. Many units built in the 1960s and 1970s, for example, put a mean single door and a couple of small windows in the wall leading on to the balcony. This kept costs down and gave occupants another slip of wall space to back the couch against. Now we might prefer a wall of glass or concertina doors to enlarge the lounge space and merge indoors with outdoors;
- playing with the **kitchen layout**—older units often have kitchens which reflect the attitudes and expectations of times past. Can you make more out of this valuable space? Do you need a traditional kitchen at all?

- adding **decorative** skirting boards, architraves and better doors;
- plastering over ugly old **ceiling finishes**;
- installing **timber floating floors** over concrete.

Yesterday's kitchen

Alice had bought an investment apartment in a good, established suburb. It was just a studio—that's all she could afford. And it was 30 years old. The previous owner, also an investor, had tidied the place up with new carpet and fresh paint, but that was the extent of it. The unit had a chequered rental history.

One problem with this studio was that it was pretty cluttered once you got a double bed and a small dining setting into the one main room. However, the kitchen was large and, importantly, a complete room by itself. The kitchen window had a great view of the city skyline and was the only part of the flat which was bathed in morning sunlight. But what had the original developer put in front of the view? The kitchen sink. The only way to enjoy the view—and the sun—was by doing the dishes.

Alice's plan was to gain access to both the view and the sun. Instead of simply replacing the old kitchen cupboards and 'updating' the surfaces, she had the space redesigned, putting a bench/table under the window in place of the kitchen sink. There were a few tricky plumbing issues, but these were eventually sorted out. She removed the old stove and installed a small double hotplate and oven unit plus a microwave, providing increased bench space. A small dishwasher went in and the large double sink became a neat single bowl.

Now there was room for two people to sit at the bench beneath the window and take in the view and sunshine as they ate their meals. It was left to the tenants to decide whether they needed a dining table at all in the main room.

Finding a technological solution

Older blocks often have lazy or under-utilised spaces, created by the designs and construction techniques of a previous era. It's here that technology can provide the missing ingredient for a financially sound redesign.

Space for the car

'It was a lovely apartment,' said Rachel, 'and in a fabulous part of Sydney's eastern suburbs, but there was no car space—and you know how valuable a car space can be! Something had to be done.'

Rachel's apartment was worth something over one million dollars but lacked the necessary off-street parking space. Clearly this would have an ongoing dampening effect on the value of her home.

There were only three apartments in the block, each one having its own floor. Underneath were two garages. 'They were old-fashioned garages, partly cut into the bedrock and partly sticking out the front of the building,' said Rachel. 'And, dating from the 1920s or thereabouts, they were out of step with modern lifestyle requirements. For example, there was no internal access to the building. You had to drive in, close the door and walk around to the front entrance. Great in the rain!'

Rachel took a good look underneath the building. Behind the two garages was a head-high cellar which was of little use to anyone. Could it be useful to her?

'There was this space below the units but it was directly behind the two garages. To make use of it you would have to sacrifice those two garages,' said Rachel. 'But I knew there was a solution using car-moving technology.

'I researched the problem and found a company which specialised in technologies for moving cars around. They only did commercial work, involving lifts and hydraulics, but I managed to get them to import a device for a domestic situation. This involved an apparatus like a slide. Worked by a remote control, it would slide a car sideways on a tray, opening access to the space behind.

'I discussed my plan with the other two apartment owners, each of whom had one of the current garages. My offer was this:

- I would push through behind the garages into the unused cellar. This would create space for four cars: two at the front, two behind them.
- I would purchase and install a car-sliding mechanism across the two front car spaces.
- Two cars could then be parked at the back, side-by-side, and one car at the front. (Only one could be at the front, on the slide, so there was room for it to move to allow a car to drive in or out from behind.)
- The mechanism would operate automatically by a remote control device—there would be no manual pushing or pulling of cars.
- In return for letting me do this, I said I would create interior access for

everyone from their car space to the foyer of the building via a new staircase. This would improve security and comfort for all owners and their families.

- In addition, I would construct individual storerooms for each unit in the remaining space at the back of the cars.
- I would also replace the existing old garage doors, which were rotting away. These old doors were operated by hand; the new ones would be automatic, with remote control.

'They both agreed to my proposal. I had the wall between the garages and the cellar demolished, put in the car slide, replaced the garage doors, then built the storerooms and the staircase to the foyer,' said Rachel. 'I covered all the costs—and did not have to pay anything else for my undercover, secured car space.

'Not only have I improved the security of the whole building, but I have got my car off the street and improved the value of my apartment. In this suburb, an off-street undercover car space is worth an extra $60 000 now—and it will be much more in the future. And the work budget was well within this.'

There's another old apartment building which is contemplating the use of car slides. Only 70 per cent of the units have a single car space, while 30 per cent have no on-site car parking at all.

The owners have come up with an interesting way of handling this difficult situation. As the building is still under company title, the company formed by the shareholders (the individual owners) controls all the car spaces and allocates them according to the company rules. Those without a current space go on a list. When someone sells their unit (the shares in the company), their car space—if they have one—passes to the next person on the list. In this way, the limited resource is shared around. Slowly.

It may have been good enough once, but that was in a different age. When the building was constructed, it's probable no one would have imagined that almost every household would have at least one car (let alone more).

The owners have now assessed the property in the light of car-movement technologies and believe they can work it so that every unit will get its own car space. Clearly this will add significant value and amenity to the building. The unaccommodated 30 per cent will bring their precious automobiles in from the cold and all will add a few tens of thousands of dollars to their balance sheets.

If you have a problem with a property or site, there may be a technological solution. Do your research and *create* your own opportunity.

Here are some examples of other technologies or new products which have changed the way we develop home units and houses:

- **door systems** which let you open up an entire wall. These are typically used in narrow houses where you can peel back the wall and enter the garden. Doors can slide into wall cavities, or simply fold upon themselves;
- split-system **air-conditioning**—a feature which is becoming increasingly desirable, particularly for bedrooms in humid towns and cities;
- **security systems**—cameras, intercoms, surveillance. Security can become a real selling feature if it is integrated into the property rather than being a clumsy 'bolt on' of mismatched bits and pieces;
- **lightweight construction materials** which allow a second storey to be built above a ground floor which was never built to take the traditional weight of a second floor;
- **inclinators** for steep sites and **elevators** for the convenience of small-block apartment owners. They can be very desirable, even though the original developers never thought they would be useful.

✓ *Tip:* An ageing population is affecting the nature and cost-benefit equation for features we can design into houses and units. What once made no financial sense might now be worthy of consideration, particularly if it creates access, privacy, security or storage solutions.

Converting common spaces to private use

There was a time when unit developments paid attention to features which could be enjoyed by all occupants. People wanted the largest backyard that could be created for the block. Now we are more concerned with privacy—we don't want to share; we would prefer a tiny private courtyard rather than a large common lawn. We have lifestyle assets which are valuable and require protection: cars, jet skis, kayaks, European cycles. When you look at your unit block, are there common areas which can be converted to private use?

- Can lockable **private storage cupboards** be built along a wall or in the yard?
- Can open car spaces be turned into **lock-up garages**?
- Can garages be extended—even going outside the existing building envelope—to provide **increased car parking** or room for private storage?
- Can the yard and/or flat roof be divided into **private courtyards** and placed on title to the individual units?
- Can you take over part of a **hallway** and relocate your front door further down the hall? I've known this to happen where the particular unit was at the end of the common hall. The extra internal space gained in this way might allow you to redesign door openings or change the floorplan of your unit.
- Is there a common **laundry** on your floor? Can you buy it from the body corporate? It might become your own private storage area or a small studio for an artist. If it abuts your unit, can you create internal access to this room?
- Does anyone use the **gymnasium**? If not, perhaps its use could be changed.
- Is the **roof cavity** sitting idle? Could this be turned into a loft or storage area?

Consider what you would have to pay the other owners for use of such an area.

If you have to make any promises, give undertakings or accept risks in return for getting necessary consent to your development, investigate taking out an insurance policy to cover you. For an investment property, the insurance might well be tax deductible too.

Use experts—an insurance broker and your accountant—to make the right arrangements so that you ensure you are covered and your costs are minimised.

Inside the roof

As she gazed at her penthouse apartment, Jenny could see little room to move. There were two bedrooms, sure, but the space was severely limited. Yet, for a range of reasons, she was going to stay where she was rather than sell up and move to a bigger home.

The top floor of the building consisted of two two-bedroom units—one was Jenny's and the other belonged to her neighbour. Jenny looked up: there was a pitched roof with a huge space inside. Could she use it?

Of course, the roof attic belonged to every owner in the apartment block. Yet it was really just wasted space, she thought. No one used it. So Jenny put a deal to her co-owners, which they accepted. She purchased the attic from the body corporate for the sum of $80 000.

She put a staircase into the attic and built three huge bedrooms and a bathroom up there. She no longer needed the two smaller bedrooms in her apartment and reconfigured the floorplan to provide larger living rooms.

The result for Jenny was an increase in value of around $300 000 to $400 000. Why?

- It was a sexy conversion—a two-storey penthouse.
- Her redesign introduced a more modern and considered style to the apartment than is typical of two-bedroom box units.
- She didn't just add more rooms—she greatly increased the size of the existing rooms (both the living rooms and bedrooms).
- There was a second bathroom.

What was in it for Jenny's fellow apartment owners? There were seven of them to persuade. If you were in their shoes, would you have agreed to sell her the attic? The general positive—in addition to the cash—was that the development was likely to impact favourably upon the building. Having a truly deluxe penthouse apartment on the top would reflect well on the value of all units. They were now in a classier block with a high-priced penthouse. Jenny's development would cost them nothing.

If anyone else had wanted to use the space, they had the opportunity to act. Indeed, Jenny had done them a favour by alerting them to the fact there was value in the unused space above their heads. But presumably they all realised they could not have a piece of the pie. It was not big enough to go around. And they were happy to get between $11 000 and $12 000 each.

As part of the deal, Jenny signed undertakings to indemnify the other owners against damage caused by her redesign—for example, water penetration. Would you give a legally enforceable undertaking like this? Don't carry the risk yourself: get a broker to arrange insurance cover for you, if you like. Pay the annual premium and don't put yourself at financial risk.

If you think your finances too tight to pay the premium, consider the average capital gain you would make, in a good location, for adding the roof space to your apartment. The cost of an insurance premium pales by comparison to what you stand to make.

Improving common assets

You don't have to make a grab for common property—in many cases, the other owners won't play ball with you. But that need not be the end of it. There is private value to be found in improving common property. And all unit owners can share in the cost. Possibilities include:

- upgrading the **foyer** with, for example, floor coverings, framed prints, designer lighting, a timber floating floor or a water feature. You can make real impact here and set the tone for the building;
- updating the interior of the **elevator** with new surfaces;
- renovating a tired **swimming pool**;
- cement-rendering ugly brick **walls**;
- making your building's **landscaping** exciting: create a sense of flow from one area to another; update the plant selection; add a fountain; install garden lighting; replace dodgy cheap tiles; add a few touches that might be too expensive if you were paying for them on your own (such as sandstone capping or retaining walls; and designer outdoor furniture;
- updating the **signage**;
- updating the **letterboxes**, particularly if they are part of a substantial piece of architecture;
- constructing an enclosure for the **garbage bins** or improving the look of the existing enclosure;
- creating a space for **bicycles** and **sports equipment**—which will get this stuff out of the building entrance and foyer;

- upgrading building **security**—newer locks, video surveillance, an automatic garage door;
- improving **communication and technology links** to pay TV, free-to-air television reception and internet access.

Converting the legal title to a more valuable form of title

Although this is not relevant to most areas of Australia, there remain pockets where apartments are not owned and regulated by a modern strata or unit title. Legally these are held under company title—a predecessor to strata title. This was a means of dividing ownership of a property within an apartment block before the law allowed separate legal titles to be created for the one piece of land. Instead of owning your unit or property freehold, you purchased shares in a company which owned all the units. By the company documents, your shares entitled you to exclusive occupation of one of the units, perhaps a car space, and common ownership of the shared spaces and building fabric.

Needless to say, company title complicates the sale and purchase of an apartment. The intricacies are not widely known and there is a degree of suspicion attaching to company title units—they are not full ownership of a unit in the way we generally understand and wish to have it. And the company articles and rules may be written so that consent is required for transfer of a member's shares into the name of a purchaser: that's a form of veto over who you can sell to.

These issues and uncertainties combine to one effect: many company title apartments sell below the value they might obtain if they were held under strata title. And here is the opportunity for investors: to persuade the shareholders to convert their title from company to strata. The process is straightforward but requires the consent of the other shareholders—check the company articles for details—as the company will have to be wound up. A surveyor and solicitor will guide you through the process, which involves preparing a strata plan and accompanying legal documents to establish titles and rights.

It should be noted that some company title buildings have achieved fame for restrictive policies and rules which are used to keep the riff-raff out—or at least silence them. Units/shares in such buildings are believed to sell at a premium and are more desirable (in certain circles) than a mere strata unit. It's not always a certain improvement in value to convert company title to strata title!

Strategies for negotiating with the body corporate

It is important to understand that not all councils will look kindly on some unit redesigns or arrangements. Check with council before launching into a project with your fellow owners—don't get everyone excited unless you know your project conforms to the planning rules and local plans. You may have to sell your idea to council too. Also confirm that you won't be breaching body corporate or strata plan by-laws. Some of these by-laws can be changed, but others can't. Your solicitor—or the body corporate's choice of solicitor—can advise you on this subject.

How will you negotiate with your fellow unit owners? It is important to find the *value* for *them*. Think in these terms:

- **Use cash**. Sometimes the best answer is the simplest. You don't need to know why someone suddenly needs some extra money, but it's not hard to get into this position. They may be having trouble at work or be thinking of retiring. They may want to pay down their mortgage or, if retired, want to travel or need to deal with family illness.
- **Give something personal**. While you have your mind on the big investment picture, it might come as a surprise that some other owners have more mundane concerns on their mind. It could be something personal such as the right to have a pet, an air-conditioner or polished timber floors—it might be necessary to amend the by-laws to allow these things.
- **Tit for tat**. If you want to convert part of the common property to an exclusive private space of your own, work out how to give others their own private slice too. Not all will want the same thing, so there could well be enough space to share around in this way. If you are having difficulty thinking what to do, you

might consider engaging an architect to sketch some alternatives so you can show other owners how it might work.

- **Talk about security**. Don't under-estimate the power of this issue. If co-owners see themselves living in their apartments into old age, they should understand the cost-effectiveness of fixing up the security of their building and property now.
- **A new area of greater use**. Can redevelopment provide the owners and tenants with something they can use? It might be the redesign of an area they don't use at present, such as a building's gymnasium. If this is under-utilised, it could become sleazy or scary to some residents, and fall into disuse and decay. If so, you have an angle for redevelopment of this common space into something more desirable.
- ***Not* having to pay cash**. From time to time, there will be areas of substantial maintenance which must be carried out. The cost per unit can be high—and some owners might not have the available funds to meet their obligations. This is a moment when the investor can perhaps offer to assist on the financial side in return for something personal or as part of a redevelopment plan for the benefit of all. See the box dealing with 'necessary maintenance' on pages 32–3.

✓ *Tip:* Find out how many of the units are occupied by owners and how many by tenants. In general, investors are less willing to spend money on redeveloping their properties until it is absolutely necessary. Small blocks filled with owner-occupiers may be easier to motivate to mutual advantage.

Before you start lobbying other owners, understand what **proportion of votes** will be required to make a change lawful. Is it a simple majority (50 per cent plus), three-quarters (special resolution) or 100 per cent of owners (unanimous resolution)? Is voting based on unit numbers or some other entitlement? The body corporate articles will set out the formula. If there is a managing agent, find out what you have to do to get your proposal on to the **body corporate agenda**. When is the next annual general meeting? Can it wait until then, or should you use the procedure to call a special meeting? As you prepare for the meeting, seek to establish how many owners have given their **proxy vote** to the managing agent. You might wish to contact other investor owners to secure their vote on your proposal or to get their proxies.

Let's go back to Rachel. She used technology to get what she wanted but, importantly, was not stingy in rewarding the other unit owners for cooperating with her plan. They enjoyed not just one benefit, but layer upon layer of improvements. Take a look again at what she offered them:

- interior access between cars and the foyer;
- improved security and comfort;
- replacement of the rotten old garage doors;
- automatic doors in place of the old manual door;
- an improved look to the building façade;
- private storerooms.

And it was offered at no cost to the others. Rachel was *generous*. But it hasn't ended there. A few years have now passed and it's time for Rachel's audacious next step. It can be hard to get fellow owners to cough up money when everything is rosy. But an expensive and pressing problem can, in an apartment block, create the impetus for joint spending on an improvement project.

Necessary maintenance—a hindrance or an opportunity to improve?

It all began when the backyard started to disappear. 'There was a small backyard which sloped away sharply. Now erosion was eating into it and we would have to build new retaining walls. They would be massive,' said Rachel. 'The quote was around $70 000 to fix the problem.'

Each unit owner was going to have to dig into their pockets and come up with something like $25 000 apiece. And for that stash of cash they would get virtually nothing—or at least nothing they would use for lifestyle improvement. It was an act of maintenance which would *hold* their property values, not extend them. This was not an enticing use of $25 000 for any of them. In particular, one of the owners could not readily put this sum together. The situation presented a dilemma for everyone.

Having already experienced the opportunities offered by a technological solution—the car slide—Rachel's two neighbours were ready to consider her next move.

'My plan was to push through the garage—under the building—into the backyard. The backyard was common property and no one really used it much anyway because of the steep slope.

'In place of the current three car spaces (two by two with one left vacant for sliding purposes), we would extend back and also *down*. Using a system of lifts, a pit and the slide, we could add no fewer than five additional car spaces down there. So there would be two levels of car spaces, accessed by automated lift and slide devices. Bear in mind that the five new spaces would be worth a combined $300 000 to the three of us.

'Because one of the three owners didn't have any money to contribute, he would get one of the new spaces while I and the remaining owner would get two new ones each (making a total of three each, with two for the non-contributing owner—a total of eight car spaces).

'The concrete works for the car spaces would tie in with a retaining system for the collapsing backyard. That pressing retaining wall problem would be solved.

'But we won't be stopping there,' she said. 'I plan to construct a rooftop garden above the new garage space. This is where the backyard is now. I may even put a swimming pool there. As part of the arrangement, the other two owners will sign over exclusive use of the garage-top garden to me. This occupies around 75 per cent of the backyard and leaves 25 per cent available for common use.

'The other contributor won't be left out of the redesign. He has the top unit, which enjoys harbour views. The roof of our building is common property and has better views. It's nice to go up there and look at the harbour, but it isn't something anyone does very often. It's simply not private enough. So the plan is to give the top owner an exclusive right to the roof area. That will become *his* private garden. Clearly that is worth a lot of money to him.'

However, much will be demanded in return for these exclusive garden areas—the redevelopment will be very expensive and will be funded by only two of the three unit owners. So this is the deal:

- The top unit gets two more undercover security car spaces, a private rooftop garden with harbour views and will save $25 000 or thereabouts which would otherwise have simply gone on a retaining wall without adding value. The total value is around $200 000. He loses access to most of the backyard—but the rooftop garden will more than compensate for this.

- Rachel also saves her 'lost' $25 000, and gets two more car spaces and a private terrace garden. Her pool will also be a desirable feature. Leaving aside the pool, the total value to her is also around $200 000. She loses access to the roof—but rarely went there anyway.
- The third owner, who is short of cash, saves his $25 000 for the retaining wall, as the other two will cover it. That's a great relief to him. He loses the use of most of the backyard and the rooftop, but wasn't using them anyway. And he gets a new undercover car space worth $60 000 at a total value of $85 000. He contributes no money to the plan, but emerges much better off.
- The estimated cost of the redevelopment is $200 000, split equally between the two contributing units. That's a spend of $200 000 to make $485 000 in added value to the three units.

'After the latest redevelopment is completed we might put in an elevator,' said Rachel. 'One of the other owners wants this, to make it easier getting from the garage to his unit and back. In return for giving my consent, I'm thinking about a little garden conservatory . . .'

✓ *Tip:* Got bad news? When the body corporate is faced with a major expense that will require a special levy from the owners, assess whether the job can be designed to add real value, not merely to fix a problem. For example, is there rust in the balconies? Do you just treat the problem or, while the scaffolding is in place, do you redesign the balconies with more contemporary materials?

Sizing up an apartment block

When inspecting an apartment, assess the unit and block to see whether there are opportunities for valuable transformation (see Table 2.1).

Table 2.1 Development opportunities: apartment blocks

Opportunity	Potential for development
Open parking	Security garaging
Vacant space indoors or in yard	Private lock-up storage
Apartment block is built into side of cliff	Excavate to create: • car spaces • improved access • storage
Common laundries	Use for: • storage • private space Is there room for private laundry facilities?
Plenty of lawn	Private courtyards
Flat roof	Convert into private courtyard(s) or add another storey?
Pitched roof	Utilise roof cavity
Tired foyer, elevator or landscaping	Redevelop to be more stylish
Poor access	Redesign with ageing population in mind: • wheelchair access • replace steps with ramps • install an inclinator or elevator • improve stairs • reduce slope of pathways • create internal access from undercover car parking to foyer
Missing out on views	• Add balconies • Move or enlarge windows • Change unit floorplan
Poor security	• Video surveillance and intercom to units • Improved locks • Improved garage door
Old-fashioned unit floorplan	Redesign floorplan to be more fashionable or useful
Old-fashioned kitchen or bathroom	Renovate to modern style, perhaps making room for internal laundry, dishwasher or other valued features
Ugly ceiling finish	Update surface
No air-conditioning	Install private split-system air-conditioning (if desirable in that location)
Cheap, nasty and worn-out doors and windows	Upgrade to raise the tone of the unit and block—it might be sufficiently effective and affordable to do this in just one room (e.g. loungeroom)

Summary

- Apartments are easily overlooked as potential development targets. There are five ways we can add value to a unit: creating more valuable spaces; finding a technological solution; converting common spaces to private use; improving common assets; converting the legal title to a more valuable form of title.
- Find the value in the deal for the other owners. Your proposal must be generous to all—don't be tempted to keep the lion's share of the profit for yourself.
- Check with council before alerting the other owners. Your proposal must be lawful.
- Check you will not breach body corporate by-laws or strata plan legislation. You may need legal advice (even if you already have body corporate support).

3

Developing a house

'The average home renovation in Double Bay is worth one million dollars,' said an architect working extensively in that part of Sydney's eastern suburbs. How is it possible to make a renovation stretch to three times the cost of constructing a decent home? Are the floor tiles made of gold and the taps turned from pieces of ex-NASA spacecraft?

According to the Australian Bureau of Statistics, there was a 36 per cent leap in expenditure on home renovation over the six years from 1995 (when we spent $2.6 billion) to 2001 ($3.6 billion). Additions, alterations and renovations now represent around 40 per cent of all borrowing for housing investment. How much more can we stuff in the envelope of our homes?

Where there's a will there's a way. Of course, this architect's comment is also a reflection of the reality that there are now parts of Australia where it is almost impossible to overcapitalise a house site. Yet the majority of our work will be in less valuable locations. Overcapitalisation is a genuine possibility, and what we decide to construct or renovate on the site will be critical to our success.

Some people look at a property and see only possibilities for what amounts to 'redecoration'; others see opportunities for far more.

The active investor's profit lies not just in decorating, but in *transforming* a property; not in simply building an extension out the back, but in *reconfiguring* the floorplan.

The classic bargain is the property which is burdened with a fatal flaw. You can buy them relatively cheaply, but what do you do next?

One 'L' of a house

When George and Bobbie went looking to buy their first house they knew only one thing: they had to live in Bondi. No other suburb would do. It was where George had spent his whole life, moving from one home to another. It was where George and Bobbie had all the memories of their first year together. They knew all the restaurants, they knew the short cuts; the circle of their common life was in that small patch of land.

But of course, being first-home buyers, they could not afford what they wanted. They had a fair bit of money behind them, however, so these were the choices open to them:

- a three-bedroom apartment in a fairly ordinary 1970s block, with half-decent district views or a water glimpse;
- a two-bedroom traditional semi, unrenovated, dark and gloomy, with no garage or secure off-street parking;
- an excellent one-bedroom apartment with good views and secure parking;
- a three-bedroom disaster of some kind, possibly with off-street parking.

After weeks spent gazing into real estate agents' windows, they were drawn towards number 4: the disaster. This was the place with potential. It was a small, two-storey terrace with a strip of land down the side. Some time in the 1960s or 1970s, the owners had built a single-storey extension to the main house, which ran along the side and occupied this yard. The development gave this small, worker's terrace a fine loungeroom and, behind, a large bathroom. These were two features rarely found in such small terrace houses.

But the place looked awful. From the street the house looked like a capital 'L'—two storeys were mated to the single-storey extension alongside. For this reason, the owners were finding it difficult to sell.

It was the extra bedroom (three instead of an otherwise affordable two) that made the place attractive to George and Bobbie. Off-street parking, plus the large lounge and bathroom, were valuable bonuses.

But it was the potential for development which really sold the property. Although they didn't have the cash when they bought it, they knew that once they had settled and got on top of the mortgage repayments they could improve the house substantially. If they could build on top of the 1960s/70s side extension, they would complete the façade of the property as a double-fronted terrace.

This is precisely what they did—although it took more years than they initially intended before they could afford to start building. They built a huge master bedroom and ensuite above the underlying lounge and bathroom. By scouring the wreckers' yards they were able to find windows, doors and wrought iron features which matched the nineteenth century part of the house.

The illusion was complete. From the street, the home was a double-fronted terrace, while inside there were large, modern, light-filled rooms which would never have existed in such a humble dwelling. At auction, the property sold easily for a healthy profit.

Catching the 'lame ducks'

Much that is written about property improvement remains stuck in an outdated, cheapskate view of the marketplace:

> We bought this old duplex and replaced the knobs on the kitchen cupboards with quirky, fashionable ones, then painted the rooms off-white apart from a feature wall in the lounge, which we changed to vermilion. In the bathroom we painted the tiles white and replaced all the taps. The new apricot chipboard vanity completed the make-over.

You might make a few dollars out of this, but you are missing the big game. Or perhaps you have bought the wrong property. Real estate agent Geoff Stean, who works extensively on development projects, offers this tip: 'In some of the capital cities smart property investors have got into "lame duck" properties, but there are many areas waiting to be discovered.'

What's a 'lame duck' property? According to Geoff: 'So many purchasers want to buy "heritage".'

> They're looking for Edwardian, Federation or California bungalow. They want something special and interesting. But they can't find them

> or perhaps they can't afford them. Investors are targeting properties for redevelopment which will appeal to these customers who can't afford their first choice.
>
> From the mid-1950s to the mid-1970s, Australians were building homes which are now right out of fashion. They are triple or double-fronted, brick veneer cottages; the bricks are all a particular shade of yellow or red. Thin metal railings run along verandahs. There's *always* a rubber plant in a pot beside the front door—I can see it now! These are what I call the lame duck houses. There are thousands of them.
>
> These provide special opportunities to the investor. Compared with renovating a heritage property—double-brick walls, plaster coatings, fragile ceilings, rising damp, difficult plumbing—the lame ducks are relatively easy to work on. And much cheaper to renovate—you can spend a lot less money to 'get it up' than on fixing a period home. After all, you're only dealing with brick veneer. Generally they were well built, too.
>
> Their value is under-estimated in locations where they are surrounded by heritage or other quality homes. It's up to the investor to appreciate their potential.

One of the common treatments for the lame ducks is to go 'Tuscan', with cement render, tiled courtyards and citrus gardens. Pulling down a couple of internal stud walls creates an open-plan lounge and dining area; you can then lose the smallest bedroom and add an ensuite and walk-in robe for a massive master bedroom complex. Profit is in the floorplan.

It can also work to choose a contemporary look for your redesign. 'Keep an eye out for new building products,' Geoff advises. 'For example, there is a sheet which looks like cement render which you can use to overlay a poor surface. Unlike older treatments, this one is quite thick and feels solid to the touch or when you tap it.'

In Geoff's regional city, investors are buying the lame ducks for around $150 000, adding $70 000 to $80 000 in improvements, then selling the new-look homes for $250 000 to $300 000. 'New kitchens, polished floorboards, all sorts of things help,' he notes. 'But one of the key tricks to the transformation is getting the colour scheme right—inside and out.'

✓ *Tip:* Don't be afraid to seek the assistance of a colour scheme expert or an interior/exterior designer. If you get it wrong, your Tuscan transformation will just look like a daggy old home which has been cement-rendered to hide the terrible cracks! Or your 'designer loft apartment' will stop short of the cutting edge, resembling an outtake from a furniture catalogue.

Strategies for renovation

Where do you want to go stylistically with your development/ renovation project? If you've decided to take the property more upmarket, what is worth doing? A number of current trends run counter to conventional wisdom, and this is where we find our redevelopment strategies. Design with the trends in mind—they are often the outward signs of lifestyle needs and desires. As such, they have emotional pulling power which helps investors to find tenants and buyers.

House trends which present opportunities for development

- **Cement bagging and painting the outside brick**. This used to be a complete no-no: investors and landlords hate painted surfaces on the outside of buildings because of the high cost of repainting at a later date. But in the heated property markets of recent years it seems this rule has been fatally breached. In no small part, this is because the paint and cement are covering ugly surfaces, such as bare cement or dark brick. Cement allows the developer to unite a number of disparate construction elements into a more pleasing whole. Add the quasi-Georgian dimension it brings to the façade and the mix is pleasing as well as valuable.
- **Minimising the kitchen so that there is more space for living**. Hands up those who saw this one coming? From bed-sit/studio apartments to three-bedroom Victorian terraces, I've known

this to happen successfully. You reduce the kitchen to the size of a single row of cupboards. No stove or oven, just a microwave, a small hotplate unit (two plates), a sink and a small preparation area. You push it against a wall and either leave it as is or use shutters and screens to put the kitchen out of sight. The reward? You get a dining table and chairs as well as a decent-sized lounge-room where once there was only room for one or the other but not both. We are becoming a nation of reheaters of food rather than home cooks (despite the proliferation of cooking shows on TV and their accompanying tomes). Or we are using just a wok or an electric grill.

- **Stacking as many garages as possible at the front**. The car is king. And when it comes to retirees, that extends to the car, the caravan and possibly the boat and jet ski. Families might have four cars where 30 years ago they had one or two. The other day I saw a house in an ordinary street with six rollerdoor garages lined up across the front. Say goodbye to any pretensions to style! The more junk we own, the more places we need to put it—preferably off the street and under lock and key.
- In fact, we are **changing the orientation of homes to the street**. In the past, a good house 'addressed' the street, with a fine frontage to impress the neighbours and formal living/dining rooms at the front. Our homes separated the part we showed visitors and the part we actually lived in. Room uses were duplicated, even in suburbia. Now, however, the design looks inwards, turning a blind eye to the street and focusing living areas towards the courtyard or lawn and pool. The implication for a renovation/redesign program is to put up big fences and create private spaces. Find the **focus point** for the house block—a place for family and friends to gather in comfort and ease—and design outwards from there.
- **To each their own bathroom**. It was obvious from the start that an ensuite off the main bedroom was a winner, but now we get home units with a separate bathroom for each bedroom. I first saw this in units built across the road from a major university. The two-bedroom unit came with two bathrooms, two secure car spaces and two lockable storage areas—perfect for a student rental market. Consider the 'bathroom' needs of the property

you are developing or renovating. Should you enlarge a bathroom, add an ensuite to the main bedroom, or sacrifice an existing room or corner of a room to provide a second bathroom for the house?

- **Adding lots of storage space**.
- **Blurring the line between house and garden**.
- **Creating open-plan living**, with fewer internal walls and pokey rooms.
- **Making multi-purpose rooms**—for example, a study which is also the guest bedroom and a 'media' room for electronica and the internet, or a bathroom which is also the laundry.
- **Going up . . . or down**—add an attic conversion, a second storey or a basement level instead of the traditional extension out the back.

✓ *Tip:* According to the Archicentre, the most important priority for renovation remains the kitchen. This doesn't mean we, as investors, have to replace it and get the latest benchtops—for we are likely to miss the mark with potential purchasers' wants and fantasies. But we should be looking at how we can create a wonderful kitchen *space*, opening walls and pushing around the floorplan to deliver an open heart to the home. If you only have the money to do one major thing, this is not a bad bet.

Table 3.1 Where should the development go?

GOING UP		GOING DOWN		GOING OUT	
pros	**cons**	**pros**	**cons**	**pros**	**cons**
Potential views	$$—very expensive per square metre	Large available space	$$$—the most expensive form of extension	$—the cheapest way to add house space	Council might have a policy against increasing the footprint of the building
Can be built within current roofline, preserving historic façade or to avoid overshadowing neighbours	Where will you put the stairs? Simple attic conversions can get by with a pull-down ladder, but not larger upstairs addition—space must be sacrificed	Does not affect neighbours' views	Uncertain timeframe for excavation—therefore cost is unknown for budgeting purposes	Level access throughout house—particularly appealing to retirees, people with a disability and landlords	Eats up the backyard and limits potential for extra car parking or a pool—both of which are valuable features
A well-designed staircase adds drama to the house layout—an emotional pull	Major disruption to downstairs level—expect some water damage and wrecked ceilings, carpets, etc.	Does not overshadow neighbours or your own backyard	Drainage issues; water penetration risk; waterproofing cost		Consider carefully what a long, thin extension will do to the flow of the floorplan

Adding a new storey provides a good opportunity to update a tired roof (e.g. worn-out tiles, lifting iron sheets)	Expect neighbour objections based around noise, overshadowing, bulk, privacy (overlooking) and loss of views	Good location for isolating noisy or less attractive rooms (e.g. rumpus room, home office, laundry, security garaging)	Ventilation; fire exit issues; light and air
	Creates areas of expensive ongoing maintenance (e.g. clearing gutters, painting timber, fixing roof leaks)		Real potential risk of causing damage to a neighbour's property; ensure your legal liability is covered and expect neighbour objections
	Ensure your existing house has the structural strength to take a second level		
	Will the design be appealing or look disunified?		

Most of our thinking about renovations and extensions focuses on the *receiving* side of the equation: an extra room, more space, taking more of the backyard. But sometimes the best solutions start with a preparedness to *give up* something.

Remember, 'development space' is not just in the backyard—it is all around the house: up, down, in and out.

Expanding the floorspace, shrinking the footprint

It was a little pocket of a suburb which was appreciating in value rapidly. Less than 100 metres away was an inlet of Sydney Harbour. Yet the suburb had pretty much languished for 30 years. Now it had been rediscovered.

Jack and Rhoda had purchased their little timber cottage before the property boom of the late 1990s/early 2000s and had a modest mortgage. They could now afford to develop the property to its potential.

First, they took their weatherboard worker's shack and wrapped verandahs around the front and the back, put in a garage, replaced the concrete-tiled roof with metal Colorbond, modernised the interior and ended up with a 1960s weatherboard bungalow. It was modernised but still had that timber charm.

Yet they wanted more. Prices soared and Jack and Rhoda could see there was little danger of overcapitalising. In fact, it was better to act now rather than wait for construction costs to increase or council standards to make development more difficult.

But the house and garage already occupied most of the site—a 460 square metre block. Indeed, there was very little landscaping and almost no yard. You could not swing a cat, let alone a cricket bat.

'We wanted to give the house more useable space, extra car parking and take the style one step further: to a San Francisco Victorian-era timber cottage,' said Rhoda. 'This period would work well, we figured, with the harbourside location. And although most of the neighbouring properties are concrete or brick, we felt our timber cottage would stand out as something more charming.'

What they wanted to do would certainly be an overuse of the site—one which would cause serious concern to council. Their solution was neat—they would give with one hand and take back with the other. Essentially, they would add more developed space while actually *reducing* the footprint of construction on the site.

'We added an upper storey of bedrooms then demolished the garage and slid the new garages *under* the house. We ended up with pretty much the maximum allowable size of house (230 square metres) plus verandahs and garaging of a further 110 square metres,' said Rhoda. 'The garage occupied 81 square metres, which was double the normal garage space you could expect in our neighbourhood for a block of this size.

'The tricky part was how to put the garage underneath the house, as it is built into the side of a hill. We engaged an engineer who prepared plans which, as it turned out, could not possibly work. I believe he never actually came to the site and inspected it—he had not taken into account just how close the neighbour's house was. His proposed method for supporting the house could not be accommodated—the neighbour's house could have collapsed.'

Ordinarily this would not be a good move. Here, however, was a dangerous twist: their neighbour was the mayor.

In the end, they went from using a tertiary-educated professional to an untrained but practical 'expert'.

'We solved the problem with the help of a house remover. He used steel beams and railway sleepers to slide long RSJ beams under the house and support it while rock was cut out below and the existing foundations were demolished.'

The house hung out from the hillside, resting on these beams and timber sleepers, for many months. The rock excavation, which was originally estimated (and costed) for ten days of work eventually lasted 36 days—at $1000 per day. A tidy overrun for the budget. Still, the result is a house which has doubled in size, doubled in garaging and yet substantially reduced its footprint on the land. Council was happy, and the neighbours were on-side too.

Overcapitalisation: Know your market

Why do we have 'slum landlords' who allow their properties to remain in a shocking condition? People still rent them, however. As a lawyer, I saw the complaints come in:

- 'I'm getting electric shocks from the stove.'
- 'When it rains, water streams down the inside of the bedroom wall.'

- 'My child is asthmatic and the bedroom walls are covered in fuzzy mould.'
- 'There is no lock on the front door.'
- 'There is a large hole in the loungeroom floor and I keep falling through it.'
- 'You can see from the bathroom into the garden—through the crack in the wall.'

What do all these dwellings have in common?

- They were in poor condition.
- Their rents were low for the area.
- They were currently rented.

An investor must have a feel for the kind of person who will become his or her tenant or purchaser. Every city and town has suburbs or small sections where people want to live, *almost irrespective* of the condition of the property they can afford. The people want to live *there.* They want to pay the *cheapest* rent possible. And to do so, they are prepared to put up with many inconveniences in the property itself.

Everyone has their own idea about what renovations strike pay-dirt and which ones are unnecessary. This explains why over-capitalisation is such an issue—we don't agree on the basics. The only rule I know for sure is this: If you ask a real estate agent: 'Should I renovate my property before putting it on the market?' he or she will answer: 'No. Let me sell it *now* for you.'

Magazine articles often list the renovations which add big value and those which don't. The majority of these are based on generalisations:

- 'Put in a new kitchen.'
- 'Put in a new bathroom.'
- 'Paint the place in neutral colours.'
- 'Pull out the carpets and sand the floors.'

I am a renovation sceptic. The property developer doesn't start with ideas about design and surface finishes, important as they may be. The developer begins with a clear understanding of the **target market** for the property.

- Who will the buyers be?
- Who will the renters be?
- How much can they afford to pay?
- What is their age?
- What are their family circumstances and living arrangements?
- Will the likely owner live in the property or use it as an investment?
- Is the property in an ethnic or cultural ghetto? If so, does this impose conditions on the renovation?
- What level of security will they require?
- How many car spaces?
- Will they want a grass lawn or will a private courtyard be preferable?
- What level of quality do they expect?
- Will they be purchasing the property because it is presented in a completed form, or are they looking for potential for further redevelopment and enhancement?

Occasionally you can spend your money on developing a property in a particular style and manage to get it just right for your buyer. In an investment/rental situation, it has been made easier over the first part of this decade by an almost slavish attention to the demands of fashion. High-quality apartment rentals had a checklist: stainless steel somewhere in the kitchen, European appliances, granite benchtops, white cupboards, halogen lights, floating laminate timber floors over the concrete slab, and so on.

The pervasiveness of lifestyle TV and home design magazines/websites, along with powerful advertising campaigns, set the tone. And who was to argue? The 'safe bet' had been defined for the property developer and the buyer/landlord.

This has highlighted the need for the developer to *complete the job*. Partial renovation will be a money trap if you fail to attract a class of buyers (or tenants) who are willing to pay more than the property is worth today.

If you completely upgrade the kitchen but the rest of the house is stuck in the 1970s, will you satisfy those who are ready to pay for a home that fits their finer lifestyle *now*? Or have you left them with too much to dislike? The tenant who is willing to pay the highest rent could probably afford to buy a home if they were so motivated. They want to live in a place which is of the standard (or location) to which they aspire but which, perhaps, they cannot afford. Unevenness of presentation and fittings (appliances, quality of tiles and carpets, etc.) turns them off the property: they can't imagine themselves living there.

✓ *Tip:* Aim to renovate so as to lift the entire property up to a new price level. Don't fiddle with a property but then leave it straddling two price points.

Lifting the *whole* property to a new level

'Our bedroom is just so small,' said Yong, who had purchased a home with her partner because of its view rather than the size or practicality of its rooms. 'We've got to do something about it.'

Indeed, when the real estate agent first showed them the property he led them in through the front door and ran over to shut the door to the master bedroom. 'We'll save this for last,' he told them. He knew it was the weakest point of what was otherwise an outstanding property.

'By the time we'd walked around the garden, admired the view and seen the number of bedrooms, we were convinced we had to have the place,' said Yong. 'So when the agent finally let us in to see the main bedroom we were already sold. Yes, it was small and had a tiny ensuite bathroom, but we were prepared to overlook these shortcomings. In fact, the "walk-in-robe", behind the bathroom, was nothing of the sort. It had a fair amount of hanging space but it was only just a "stand-in" robe.

'After buying the home and living in it for some time we felt we would have to do something about the small main bedroom. Right behind that room was a double garage—we knew the most economical solution would be to push through into the garage, make it the master bedroom, and punch a doorway into the existing ensuite. It would give us a massive new bedroom—a real asset which would add considerable value.

'The old main bedroom would become an office or an interesting little lounge area as an extension of the bedroom complex. In so doing, the stand-in robe would be retained, for use as a place to put office files or to store out-of-season clothes, jackets, ski gear and the like.

'We'd build a new garage for the cars. It would be much cheaper to move the garage than to build on a large new bedroom somehow connected to the main roof of the building.'

Yong and her partner drew their sketches and liked the way the plan was coming together. They showed these to a draftsman who basically agreed they were doing the right thing but offered no great insights. He said: 'Yeah—let's go with it!' They felt he wasn't the right man for the job.

A second draftsman suggested a change to the plans.

'He recognised that it was a valuable property which could support a good, well-designed home. He said we would need a larger ensuite bathroom if we were to complete the upgrade brought about by having a large master bedroom. "But we don't want to spend a lot of money moving the ensuite plumbing—and where would it go anyway?" we said.

'His recommendation was to extend the current ensuite into the robe area behind it. This, he said, would give a larger ensuite so we could have a shower big enough for two people plus a set of double basins along the wall.

'We realised at once he was right,' said Yong. 'The new master bedroom was going to be a wonderful space but the pokey ensuite bathroom would then be out of character. You could see a prospective buyer's eyes light up when they first saw the bedroom, then watch them dim as they squeezed into the ensuite. We were solving one problem but merely deferring the disappointment.

'Yes, we would have to forgo the usefulness of the robe area for holding office files or winter clothes, but they could always go elsewhere. The lesson for us was to be prepared to sacrifice a minor feature for the opportunity to make an impact while maximising a much more important one. Our home will now appeal to a whole new segment of buyers.'

What value did the walk-in robe have? Had that value diminished once it was no longer attached to the master bedroom? Yong got a 40 per cent increase in the size of her ensuite bathroom. The ensuite would match the level of luxury she was creating for the main bedroom.

When you get into active, hands-on property investment, you are working with a broader horizon than as a passive property investor. In assessing a property for acquisition or development, you are looking beyond current yield and expected capital growth for *this* property—you are looking for the potential yield and potential capital growth of this property after you have reshaped it.

A house, for example, could be reshaped to fit the needs of several customer profiles: one residence or multiple dwellings, commercial or industrial, home business, cottage or mansion, period home or modern décor.

Scenario: you are assessing an inner-city terrace house for purchase and redevelopment. It is classic Victorian in features, although the upstairs balcony has been filled in with timber and glass in place of the original wrought iron. The house comprises three levels: two bedrooms at the top, two formal rooms and a bathroom on the ground level (front entrance) and, below, a kitchen, laundry with bathroom, lounge and dining. A bland rectangular room has been added in the backyard—it was used as a storage facility by the current owner, who ran a small business from the house. The yard has room for two to three cars or a garden.

So what are the development alternatives?

1 **Keep it as a small office with an attached residence**. In this part of the city you can expect good capital growth, so don't spend a dollar more than you have to. What you will gain in rent will never outstrip the passive capital gain, so keep your costs low. The problem, however, is twofold: the property in its current configuration only appeals to a small section of the market. It is not a great house. Second, rental income as proportion of the value of the property is very low—around 3 per cent. So it is costly just to own.
2 **Turn it into a nicer home**. One of the great drawbacks of this property as a home is that there is no bathroom on the bedroom level. It is hard to calculate what an ensuite would add to the value of the property in dollar terms, but it would certainly give it wider appeal. This house is not cheap any more—and those with the means of buying a good inner-city terrace house are going to want certain comforts for their money. They will not want to be descending the steep stairs in the middle of the night. An ensuite could be built on top of the ground floor bathroom (which juts out the back of the house) or the small second bedroom on the upper level could become a changing room and ensuite. Other bedrooms could be added on the garden level in the rectangular room near the kitchen.

3 **Increase the yield by converting the house into two apartments.** This three-storey terrace has two ground-level entrances—a major feature for development purposes. The house could be split so that the two top floors (with access from the street) were separated from the lower ground floor (with access from the rear lane). Both apartments currently have a bathroom and bedrooms (or space suitable for conversion to bedrooms). Only one level has a kitchen, but it would be possible to build on top of the garden rectangle room, providing a kitchen and dining room for the upper apartment. There is car parking for both apartments—another key factor in assessing a property for development.

   The yield from the property would jump sharply by having two tenancies. It also grants you a reduction in overall financial risk because you are not relying on a single occupancy to pay a substantial rent in support of your mortgage and outgoings. However, if you created two apartments, would you make it too difficult and expensive for a future owner to turn the property back into a single upmarket home? Would you be limiting your appeal to various categories of customer? This is the dilemma. The androgynous nature of the property in its current form arguably holds back its full potential value, but also means that purchasers and tenants with different needs can see in this property a bit of what they may want.

4 **Demolish the back half and redesign specifically for your chosen market**. Pull down the bathroom and the rectangular garden room. Rebuild over two or three storeys, either to turn the house into a residential mini-mansion or to make it a better property for commercial use. The sizeable rear yard, with its capacity to take two or three cars, is a valuable and rare asset for an inner-city terrace. Many of the earlier renovations of this sort of property involved a fairly basic extension into the rear yard—cheap and inefficient in design. They hold the property value back. If you chose to take the terrace further upmarket, as a home, you would do well to consider getting rid of these 1970s/80s extensions and starting again.

Which development would you choose? It all comes down to your marketing plan.

Marketing strategies which drive renovation

When you have a clear idea of who you want to rent (or sell) the property to, the style and nature of renovations becomes clearer. Table 3.2 shows some sample strategies to consider when assessing a house for development. To a degree, these are caricatures of reality but you can see how easy it becomes to waste money on renovation and redesign—once you head off in a particular direction you start to negate a number of other possibilities for the property.

Obviously you will have your own views on the matters listed in the table. What is important is that you know your target market (or markets) and renovate with this in mind. This is the foundation for avoiding overcapitalisation.

Table 3.2 Strategies to consider when developing a property

Target market	Buyer or tenant?	Lifestyle issues	Design implications
Young student; young employed; middle-aged under-employed	Tenant	• Out a lot • Low maintenance • Little interest in gardening or cooking • Require inexpensive accommodation	• No garden—a small courtyard will do • Small kitchen—no need for traditional full-sized stove • Cover floors with basic carpet and vinyl (cheap and simple to clean)
Family with children	Buyer	• Lots of time spent at home • Need outdoor space for kids • More than one car • Cook at home	• Incorporate heating and cooling appliances or systems (where appropriate) • Large kitchen • Backyard with at least some lawn • If extending the building into the backyard, try to leave space for a future swimming pool • At least one lock-up garage plus off-street parking for another car

Target market	Buyer or tenant?	Lifestyle issues	Design implications
			• More than one bathroom • Private area for parents' retreat, home office • Consider installing some timber flooring to highlight rugs and furnishings • Fix structural problems
Family with children	Tenant	• Lots of time spent at home • Need outdoor space for kids • More than one car • Cook at home • Low maintenance	• Incorporate heating and cooling appliances or systems (where appropriate) • Large kitchen—in an upmarket home the tenant will appreciate fashionable design elements here • Backyard with at least some lawn • More than one bathroom • At least one garage or carport and, ideally, good on-street parking • Cover floors with basic carpet and vinyl (cheap and simple to clean)
Retiree	Buyer or tenant	• Likely to be away from home for extended periods • Strong requirement for personal security • Seeks privacy • Caravan or boat storage • Gardening and hobby pursuits • Disability • Seeking easy, low cost maintenance • Widely varying levels of income	• Build security into the premises: good locks, bars, security screen doors, peepholes, intercom, video; it should be easy to lock the place up and disappear for weeks at a time • Design with disabilities in mind: non-slip flooring, handrail in bathroom and for stairs, taps which are easy to grip and turn, ramps, remove obstacles and hazards

Table 3.2 continued

Target market	Buyer or tenant?	Lifestyle issues	Design implications
			• Don't create expensive future maintenance traps—such as polished timber floors throughout • Some will want a small, private, low-maintenance courtyard; others love to garden or need space to work on hobbies and projects • Secure off-street accommodation for car and possibly caravan/ boat • One bathroom might be sufficient
Couple, no children	Buyer	• Out a lot • Dinner parties at home • Working long hours • Prepared to work hard to make home suit their lifestyle aspirations • Little disposable income while paying the mortgage	• Requires impressive space for entertaining—could be courtyard, garden, deck, lounge/dining room • Will be assessing properties for renovations they can do later themselves to customise the home to their tastes and to save some money on the purchase price • Will want their own kitchen design and will not want to pay extra for yours (unless, by chance, it is a perfect fit) • Need a good main bedroom • Incorporate some touches to forge an emotional connection with your buyer—e.g. timber flooring, water feature in

Target market	Buyer or tenant?	Lifestyle issues	Design implications
			garden, leadlight panel somewhere • One bathroom might be sufficient
Couple, no children	Tenant	• Out a lot • Dinner parties at home • Working long hours • Possibly with higher level of disposable income (rent is cheaper than a mortgage)	• Require impressive space for entertaining—could be courtyard, garden, deck, lounge/dining room • Needs a good main bedroom • Modern kitchen • Low-maintenance, hardy garden • Cover floors with basic carpet and vinyl • One bathroom might be sufficient
Investor	Buyer	• Bargain hungry • Borrowing a lot of money • Keen to minimise vacancy risk • Considering tax consequences: looking at depreci-ation of building and fittings • Looking at the potential of the property—to renovate, demolish or extend	• Must be ready to rent—ideally has a tenant in place • Low-maintenance surfaces and few inbuilt appliances • New hot water service; good basic stove (wary of fashionable appliances which can be expensive to repair) • Dislikes swimming pools, painted outside walls, rising damp, old ceilings, dodgy wiring and plumbing • Low-maintenance garden or, preferably, a paved courtyard—no gardening • A basic kitchen—not a fashionable one which will date quickly or require maintenance to look good • More than one bathroom is desirable for

Table 3.2 continued

Target market	Buyer or tenant?	Lifestyle issues	Design implications
			maximising rent from share households • Consider whether there is a chance the purchaser will demolish the property
Small business	Tenant	• Level access • Parking • Security • Storage • Low maintenance yard • A number of office spaces	• Courtyard instead of garden • Don't fill the yard entirely with car spaces—workers will need a place to sit outdoors • Bars on windows, security shutter doors, intercom • Install wiring for basic office communications equipment • Air-conditioning and heating—split-system units or a ducted system • Kitchen can be compressed • Are two bathrooms needed? • Are the bedrooms suitable for use as offices or will you have to change doorways or the floorplan?

A safety plan

Safety is a key issue. Whatever else you fail to do with your investment property, never neglect safety and insurance. This is particularly important when renovating and upgrading a property—indeed, some states have legal requirements about the installation of smoke detectors, for example. Discuss the safety issue with council officers while you are working on your plans.

When renovating your property, consider creating a safety plan. Get experts to check and confirm the building is safe for occupants and ensure that it complies with all conditions placed on development and construction approvals. Address your liability issues and manage the risk. Consider these measures, where appropriate, in your development plans:

- fire exit signs;
- fire-rated doors and surfaces;
- fire escapes;
- sprinkler systems;
- smoke detectors;
- good lighting;
- safe stairs;
- safe electric and gas appliances and services (pipes, wiring, meters, fuse boxes, circuit boards, power points, etc.);
- earth leakage safety switches;
- appropriate and working locks on external doors and windows where necessary;
- security screen doors;
- removing poisonous plants and potentially hazardous trees (falling limbs, etc.) from the yard;
- other 'falling' hazards: chimneys which are no longer supported inside the building (brickwork removed), unsafe retaining walls and fences;
- safety glass in bathroom doors, shower screens and low windows/doors;
- ventilation in bathrooms, kitchen and laundry;
- effective termite barriers and other pest prevention strategies;
- slippery floor tiles and surfaces;
- floor coverings which have lifted edges;
- rising damp;
- mould due to water penetration from roof or window frames, etc.

The business of creating solutions

Geoff and Anna owned a large, double-brick three-bedroom home in Sydney. It suffered from rising damp in a huge front room—

almost like a mini-ballroom in style—and for a couple of metres down the wall of the adjacent hallway. Very nice place, shame about the damp.

Wishing to sell the home, they got a number of experts to assess the problem and realised they had to install a damp course. There are various technologies on offer to deal with this and they had no difficulty choosing the one they wanted and could afford.

The job was duly done and ticked off their pre-sale list of 'things to do'. They waited a couple of months before repainting the plaster on the brick walls. 'The walls were completely dry when we painted,' they told me. 'They had been dry for weeks. So we saw no harm in pressing ahead.'

Within a couple of weeks, after a rainy spell, damp marks shone through the new paint. And the dank smell returned too; together with little crystals.

They had been advised that they should remove all plaster that had once been wet and wait many months before redecorating. There was moisture still in the wall and it needed time and exposure to dry out properly. Their impatience had resulted in there being no solution at all to the damp problem.

I once went to an open house inspection for a home with charming big old timber windows. But when I tried to open one, I found it would not budge. I asked the agent what the problem was and he said: 'It's only paint—it's been painted over. Easily fixed with a razor blade.'

He was wrong. Upon closer inspection I could see that parts of the timber frame had been packed with plastic filler and then painted over. Presumably there had been wet or dry rot in the frame. Rather than get a carpenter to cut out the bad timber and replace it with good timber, the owners had gone for a 'quick fix' that, in fact, fixed nothing.

Would a bodgy window like this worry you or put you off buying (or renting) a home or apartment? It might not; or it might lead to some kind of violence on a sultry, humid summer's night when you found you couldn't open the window to let in the breeze.

Of course, one fudged repair is usually an indicator that there will be more of its kin about. It displays a certain attitude.

In my experience, a partial fix can return to bite you on the backside, costing money and, often more importantly, delay. Yet many tradespeople and builders seem set on 'ticking jobs off a list' rather than fully solving the problems of the property. The new door is affixed with four screws instead of twelve (two on the top hinge, two on the bottom); the new shutters are on the wall, but don't meet properly when closed; the reverse-cycle air-conditioning has been installed, but it makes the wall vibrate when switched on; they've dealt with the rain water which was pooling at the garage door—and now it pools at the front doorstep; the roofing man put the obviously slipped tile back in place and told you to get the ceiling repaired, only for you to realise that water was getting in from more than one spot in the roof.

Gain 100 per cent more garden and 30 per cent more home

'Our home was at the bottom of a tall cliff,' said Colette, 'about 6 metres down below the main road. A narrow path wound along a ledge to reach our single car space.

'But our house was in an expensive suburb, where owners would expect something a bit better than this. We knew that we would substantially increase the value of our property if we could develop it to meet the market demand.

'So we got in an excavator who worked away at the sloping cliff behind our home for *eight months*! As he chopped at the sandstone, we found we were living in a quarry! In the end he removed our small backyard—which was largely wasted space—and we constructed a four-car garage with additional living room and a laundry. Then we put a rooftop garden above the garage.

'The result was that we doubled the size of our backyard and made it all usable. And we trebled the amount of functional space offered by our home: the four-car, undercover garage, the new living room and laundry. Our new backyard was a level terrace—much better for entertaining.

'As part of the development we were able to get the roadway lowered to meet the new level we had created. Council agreed to the necessary changes because we were the last property before a dead end. What we were doing wouldn't inconvenience other properties and everyone could see how the development would improve the situation for our home.'

Measure the return in terms of additional rent

Suppose you've got a fairly typical two-bedroom home unit. It's twenty years old and not much has been done to it since it was new—it's in 'original condition' throughout. You can renovate and develop your unit's potential and maybe it will attract a higher rent. But what do the figures tell you?

Sam owns a two-bedroom unit in Ramshead worth $300 000. The tenant is about to vacate after a five-year occupancy at a rent of $260 per week. Sam wants to get the unit freshly painted and put in new carpet.

He gets the following quotes:

- painting (supply of paint and labour): $1500;
- carpet (supply and fitting): $2000.

Nothing too scary so far. He can afford this.

Sam's managing agent says the painting and new carpet will lift the expected rent for his unit by $15 per week, to $275. Sam pulls out an old envelope and does the figures on the back:

$15 x 52 weeks = $780 additional income over one year

But it's actually less than this—the managing agent takes 6 per cent ($46.80). So Sam will make $780 – $46.80 = $733.20 per year.

At that rate, the renovations ($2000 + $1500 = $3500) would be paid for by the additional rent after four and three-quarter years.

Sam is grateful he didn't opt for the new kitchen ($12 000), which would take a decade to pay off out of the extra rent it could bring to the property. (Tax deductions might help too—see Chapter 10.)

When you think about figures like these, why would you ever pay money to develop your investment property? But there are good reasons nevertheless:

- to **continue to attract tenants**—if the place looks tatty, it will be harder to find a tenant at all (and you will have to reduce or stall the rent);

- to **attract a better quality tenant**—who will appreciate and respect a well-appointed property;
- to **reduce annual maintenance and repair costs**;
- to **keep the property in condition suitable to maximise its sale value** if circumstances meant you needed to sell it swiftly (for reasons of debt control, running your business, death or illness in the family, and so on);
- to **improve your cashflow**.

This last point is one of those great hidden treasures for the property investor. Let's say you do the kitchen job, pay $12 000 and lift the rent by $25 per week. The value of the unit rises from $300 000 to $325 000 on the back of the renovation. There are three implications flowing from this. The first two are:

- you can borrow more money;
- you can afford a higher level of repayments on your loan.

Sam's unit, after installation of the new kitchen, is worth $325 000—an increase of $25 000. His bank lends him up to 80 per cent of the value of his property. Sam now wants extra funds to finance the purchase of a second investment property.

Current mortgage: 80% of $300 000 = $240 000
Potential mortgage: 80% of $325 000 = $260 000
New borrowings (using existing equity): $20 000

That's a 10 per cent deposit on a one-bedroom unit worth $200 000. The extra rent income will come close to supporting this.

So the spending of $12 000 has purchased both a kitchen and the capacity to borrow an extra $20 000. But there's one more financial benefit: you should be able to sell the property for a higher price based on cashflow alone.

Investors are not totally fixated on the price they must pay to purchase a property. They are also vitally interested in the cashflow or yield of the investment. The extra rent generated by the new kitchen, modest as it is, becomes a matter of pure maths to the investor.

Of course, in many cases it is simply not worth developing the potential of the property through renovation. The most obvious example is where the true potential of the dwelling lies in its demolition to make way for a new development. In such cases, the developer rests content with a lower rent because he or she will never see the return on investment of even a coat of paint and new carpet, let alone a kitchen makeover.

First do your sums.

Ten rules of renovation

1. See the property as a whole: aim to lift the *entire* property up to a new price level for sale or rent.
2. Do your sums, both for rent return and sale of the property.
3. Speak to your accountant while still formulating your plan—find out what work will be tax advantaged and when you will receive the monetary benefit (at the end of *this* financial year or only when you sell?).
4. Always use licensed builders and tradespeople. Check them out first.
5. Speak to council and get all necessary approvals before you start work, and any necessary certificates upon completion. These protect you from litigation and ensure you are ready to sell the property if and when you decide to.
6. Let the light in.
7. Create 'lifestyle spaces'—reconfigure the floorplan if necessary.
8. Follow current decorating fashions only if you intend to sell or rent the property soon.
9. Problem-solve the property. Aim to fix problems which affect the value or saleability of the property. Don't just fiddle around the edges: fix the structural problems.
10. Think carefully about what you can DIY and what should be left to experts.

Sizing up a house for redevelopment

When inspecting a house, assess the property for opportunities for valuable transformation.

Table 3.3 Development opportunities: houses

Opportunity	Potential for development
Open parking	Security garaging
Garage not connected to house	Undercover access between house and garage
Ugly bricks or exterior claddings	Conceal, update and unite these with cement render or new construction materials
House is built into hillside	Excavate to create: • car spaces • improved access • storage • rumpus room
Large front yard	Additional off-street parking for cars, boat, caravan, etc.
Large rear yard	• Building extension • Pool
Flat roof	• Courtyard • Add another storey?
Pitched roof	• Utilise roof cavity • Dormer windows?
Tired-looking garden and landscaping	Redevelop to be more stylish: • Parterre garden or other fashionable style of the moment • Water feature • Use of paving • Quality retaining walls • Garden lighting
Poor access	Redesign with ageing population in mind: • Wheelchair access • Replace steps with ramps • Install an inclinator or elevator • Improve stairs • Reduce slope of pathways
Missing out on views	• Add balconies • Move or enlarge windows • Change floorplan
Poor security	• Video surveillance and intercom • Improved locks • Improved garage door
Old-fashioned floorplan	Redesign floorplan to be more fashionable or useful
Old-fashioned kitchen or bathroom	Renovate to modern style, perhaps making room for internal laundry, dishwasher or other valued features

Table 3.3 continued

Opportunity	Potential for development
No ensuite bathroom to main bedroom	Add ensuite: • as separate, new room • using part or all of an existing room
No air-conditioning	Install private split-system air-conditioning (if desirable in that location)
Cheap, nasty and worn-out doors and windows	Upgrade to raise the tone of the house; it might be sufficiently effective and affordable to do this in just one room (e.g. loungeroom)
Butchered period home	Restore period features
Poor or restricted access from house to garden	Open up back of house on to the garden

Summary

- Don't just decorate, *transform*; look for ways to improve the floorplan.
- There are trends in renovation steps which pay—update your understanding of what is required.
- Know your market.
- Consider the safety of those who will occupy your development. Ensure you comply with all government standards and council-imposed conditions.
- 'Development space' is not just in the backyard—it is all around the house: up, down, in and out.
- If you plan to retain part or all of the development, measure the return on your expenditure in terms of additional rent that will be generated.
- Create solutions and fix problems.

4

Medium-density housing

Does the future still hold a revered place for the classic Aussie three-bedroom home? As we all know, the big backyard is an endangered species. Australians now prefer low-maintenance courtyards in place of lawns, the car is king and privacy/security is a great selling asset for any property. Even the two-bedroom home unit could become almost unnecessary as a staple.

Population projections from the Victorian government are of interest for all regions. These suggest the number of single-person and childless couple households in our society will almost double by the year 2031. Two-parent family households, complete with children and a dog, will fade a little (by around 2 per cent). One-parent families in Victoria will rise from 195 000 to an estimated 279 000. But the giant leap is reserved for couples without kids (up from 458 000 to an estimated 776 000—an increase of 69 per cent) and one-person households (450 000, rising by 85 per cent to 831 000).

Behind this dramatic shift are a number of lifestyle factors, as well as the simple fact that we are an ageing population. People are marrying later in life and delaying having children. We live crowded lives and crave our own private space—even if this is just a bedsit/studio apartment—rather than sharing with flatmates. An ageing population also means there is more interest in housing which can accommodate people with disabilities, arthritis and so on.

All this supports the interpretation that we will be reducing the size of homes and blocks of land. Single developments are now being built containing 2500 to 3000 apartments and houses. Green Square in Sydney has its own 'town centre' and railway station on a 487 hectare site. Rhodes Waterside is a $1 billion development with 1600 apartments and terrace homes as well as two office blocks, an eight-screen cinema centre and a major retail precinct. Note that such new mega-scale residential developments are not in the style of US gated communities—they remain open. But with the parks, movies, shops, marinas and sporting facilities, need you ever leave (other than to go to work or to visit your grandmother)?

People will accept a smaller space if the quality, location or features are more intensely attractive. We don't all need to be 'Green Square' developers—because, surely, not everyone is ready for life in such over-planned communities. Already we are seeing a widespread trend towards subdividing the big backyard to create neat, compact dwellings.

Building in the backyard

One of the main investment priorities is to get rid of the home mortgage. This provides the investor with three great advantages:

1 **personal security**;
2 elimination of **non-deductible debt** (the interest on a home mortgage is not a tax deduction);
3 **equity**, which can be used as security for investment borrowings (where the interest is tax-deductible).

For most people, this is but a dream. Our income does not match our desire to rid ourselves rapidly of the home mortgage. It will be a slow process. But some home owners are prepared to take a shortcut to mortgage-free living. Their strategy is to build a second home in the backyard then sell it and pay off (or substantially lower) their home mortgage. Similarly, by subdividing then selling off the backyard, you could finance a substantial rebuilding of your existing home.

A second dwelling might start life as a granny flat, remaining on the one legal title. If carried out with the right approvals, however, it could be subdivided at a later stage (or immediately) to create a second lot which can be sold off separately from the first. Clearly the property must have the necessary dimensions for subdivision with council approval. Sometimes owners discover this by accident, while others purchase their home with the intention of eventual subdivision.

If you intend purchasing a home with this intended investment strategy in mind, carefully consider the pros and cons (see Table 4.1).

Table 4.1 Should you subdivide?

Arguments for	Arguments against
You can make money by selling off the second block	By how much will you reduce the value of the block you keep?
You retain your home	The yard will be substantially smaller and there may be privacy issues for both blocks. You might decide you have to move out and buy elsewhere—and that will cost you tens of thousands of dollars.
You can still live fronting on to the street—it's as though nothing has changed	Consider access issues for the rear block. The owners will drive past the full length of your home whenever it suits them.
The second house will attract a premium for being brand new	The owners of the second block will know precisely where to find the developer if they wish to complain: over the fence.
You are maximising the potential of the block	You are minimising the potential of the existing house. Seek advice as to whether a substantial renovation and redesign—e.g. pool, ducted air-conditioning, new façade—would net you more money. Obtain taxation advice too.
You get to design your neighbouring house. Alternatively, you might choose to move into the new dwelling and sell the one you are living in now	You will care about the design—because you will be living in it or next door to it. This adds cost and can lead to delay. There is an emotional dimension to your investment decision-making.

The last point from this table is too easily overlooked. Simon is a bank employee in a city in Victoria who found himself caught in this exact dilemma. Through the bank, he had easy access to a construction loan on favourable terms. By accident, he and his wife had purchased a home on a block of land which was large enough to support three dwellings under council's policy and regulations. They were very keen to pay off their home mortgage and saw subdivision as the way to do it.

Having made up their minds, they quickly found a surveyor, drew up the subdivision and engaged an architect to plan the two new dwellings and the renovation of their existing home. All plans were duly approved by council. But at the construction stage the wheels ground to a halt. They found they could not communicate the more detailed aspects of the development to their builder (who had been selected on the basis of solid recommendations). They did not want to dump this one and find a different builder—he had their confidence. Yet, as they pored over the draft building plans, they kept discovering problems.

Essentially, these were problems only because Simon and his wife were going to live in one of the new dwellings. Not only was this their opportunity to kill off the mortgage, but they would get a brand-new home out of it, with all the little design features that can mean so much.

It took more than twelve months to move through this stage, to the point where construction began. Fortunately for Simon, he was able to keep his construction loan on hold even though he technically had to reapply for it as approval had lapsed. But, in investment terms, they had just wasted a year.

✓ *Tip:* Negotiate a long-term finance arrangement with your lender so that you do not have to face dealing with a lapsing of your loan approval. It could take a year to 18 months to start construction.

Going further: multiple townhouses

A multiple townhouse development is an extension of the strategy discussed earlier in this chapter. The investor might still consider living in one of the new properties, so the arguments in the table above remain relevant. Below is a case study which illustrates the rewards and the risks.

Beginner's luck . . . or smart planning?

Joy is a newspaper journalist who lives in Perth. She does not enjoy a millionaire's income. Yet she has just finished her first three-lot subdivision and has begun work on the second.

At first I thought her story was nothing more than beginner's luck. Everything went well. Too well. But on reflection it was clear that she had done her homework. Care and attention to the small things had delivered a healthy profit for two years' part-time effort. This was on top of her full-time, demanding job.

Here's how she did it. Joy already owned a house, so she had a basic familiarity with property. She knew she had little opportunity in her chosen career of making much money, so she turned to property.

The first thing she did right was to join forces with a bloke who had worked in the building industry. He would handle the builders and tradesmen while she looked after the finances, design and decorating. It was a blending of two areas of skill—he could keep the building side of things on track, while she had the interrogation and financial skills to keep the bank happy and to do all the shopping.

After looking around for opportunities in the property market, she hit upon subdivision. 'Over here in Perth there are all these areas which have large housing commission homes on big blocks of land. In fact, they are triple-sized blocks,' she said. 'The houses are run down and that keeps their value lower than it should be.

'We bought one of these old houses in an area which was starting to move ahead. Development was going on in the suburb, with bright new homes replacing all the old, tired houses. They're not everywhere—but you'll find them in small pockets.

'The one we chose to buy had a level block of land. We thought this was very important as we knew it would keep site costs down when building began.

'Our plan was to subdivide the land into three blocks and build "triplets"—three houses or villas. There was one common wall between each pair.

'From looking at the market we could see there was a real trend in the area to down-sizing. People were wanting smaller homes that offered security and were easy to look after. Lots of people were happy to live without the big backyard.

'One of the wisest choices we made was to find a helpful banker. We had a very good relationship with the bank. We decided to be totally up-front and honest with him about what we were planning to do. To his credit, the banker really supported us in the project—and knew he could rely on us.

'He lent us all the money we needed for the development—to buy the land, get the plans drawn and approved and to construct the three homes. But he went further. Perhaps realising we did not have large incomes, he even lent us the *interest* we would have to pay on the loan. This meant we didn't pay any interest on the mortgage until the houses were sold. It made everything so much easier—and more affordable.

'One of the benefits of choosing this particular type of property for subdivision was that there was still a functioning house on the land. This meant we could rent it out over the whole period when we were getting plans prepared and taking the development through council. This extra income really helped us out. Then, when building work began, we gave the tenant notice.

'And we had no troubles with council—they were very keen to see these run-down properties turned into something better. They were very proactive, helping developers turn a dingy area into a more beautiful part of the suburb.'

Joy has some advice to pass on to other would-be developers. 'First, I'd say you have to be organised.' (Bear in mind that Joy was doing much of the work at night and on the weekends.)

'Watch out for the building contract. Read the fine print.

'Don't overcapitalise. Do-it-yourself where you can. We went looking for things like ovens and sinks and purchased them ourselves. This meant we didn't have to pay the builder for these things. You can save a lot by doing the groundwork for the builder and tradespeople.

'You should also make the homes attractive, so they stand out. We added a lot of little extras that we didn't have to. For example, we put a small hand basin into the toilet, making it into a powder room by itself. And we installed air-conditioning and better quality architraves and skirting boards than you would expect in the price range of the villas.

'All this paid off quickly. In fact we sold two of the villas on the first open day. The last one sold the next day—for more than we were asking.

'We're now working on our next subdivision. It will be the same scale of project. One thing we might do differently, in the current climate, is to market and sell the villas ourselves. I don't think we need a real estate agent this time around.'

Joy still has her day job. Through good organisation, and having a complementary partner, she sees no reason to quit. She can be an employee by day and a property developer by night.

On the first deal, she estimates her expenses, including buying the property, construction, all fees, estate agent commissions and interest, amounted to almost $700 000. The gross profit, on sale of the three villas, was around $110 000. It was deceptively graceful and easy.

It can be a giant leap for a property investor to move from an essentially passive role into the active creation of a medium-density project. Be prepared for these traps:

- **Get your measurements right**. Ensure there is enough land to divide into acceptable lot sizes—with some left over. As you can understand, planning for three lots and then finding that only two will work on the site is a catastrophe of biblical proportions for most of us. Don't rely on your own maths or what the estate agent tells you: hire an expert (surveyor, architect or town planning consultant) to confirm the subdivision layout with council officers.
- **Don't rely on what has been built elsewhere**: the rules change.
- Wherever possible, **choose a level site** and consider **obtaining an engineer's report** so you will know in advance the risks of unbudgeted excavation or footings design. Building quotes are often based on the assumption that the site is ideal and the footings will be of the cheapest kind.
- Wherever possible, choose a block where neighbours will cheer you as you demolish the current buildings. Find out where council would love to see you improve the streetscape.
- If you have any doubts about your ability to handle the builders, get in someone to cover this part of the turf. Sure, you'll be splitting the potential profit. If it goes well, next time you might be able to handle it all yourself. But if you try to do everything on your own, there might not be a next time.
- **Be organised**. If you are working full time, get a 'runner'—someone to pick up the taps and stoves or visit the construction site for you. You can't do it all. Delay costs money.
- **Save costs on things you can easily do yourself**: choosing tiles, fixtures and fittings, floor coverings, appliances, skirting boards and architraves, door handles, doors, etc.

- **Find a mortgagee who understands what you are trying to do** and who is constructive about how to finance this.

I would add the clear warning that what Joy did was financially very risky. Borrowing the principal plus the interest is a dangerous strategy which I would not recommend. Yet Joy had done much to lower her risk at key points. In particular, she had addressed the black hole which can appear in the construction phase. It is critical that there be no serious dispute with your builder and no lengthy delay—for any reason. How can you guarantee it will proceed smoothly? You can't. But it will help to have someone on your team who has worked with your builder before and/or who knows where to anticipate problems and how to prevent them turning into a communication breakdown or Mexican stand-off.

Medium-density guidelines

If you are contemplating a development which creates multiple dwellings—townhouses or some flats behind an old house on a large block of land—get hold of council's guide to medium-density housing and read it before you instruct your designer/architect. If you haven't seen one of these documents, you will be surprised at the breadth of matters which councils require to be taken into account in the drawings. In many ways, these are way beyond what is required for a common home renovation.

The language is no longer merely bureaucratic. There is a strong concern to drive home the point that council will look at the plans with an eye to the *spirit* of what it wants, not just the letter of the law. You'll find statements of principle like this:

> *Design your medium density housing (MDH) development to be a HOME. The neighbourhood around your MDH development is comprised of people's HOMES. WOULD YOU LIVE IN YOUR MDH DEVELOPMENT?* [Their capitals, not mine.]

Gradually, this policy has resulted in an extraordinary number of planning conditions or expectations which add considerably to the cost of development and the difficulty of taking a straight path through the approvals process. This is not something I object to—I'm all in favour of more livable, friendly development. But the hurdles must be identified right from the commencement of the development process if heartbreak and dyspepsia are to be avoided.

The guidelines are extensive and vary according to the council and state/territory. It's a simple matter to get hold of a copy for your site and you can read all about it in detail. For now, I would like to show you the flavour of these medium-density guidelines so you can start to think about how they might impact on your plans.

- Council doesn't want you to build an MDH development in a **short court** or a **dead-end street**, in part because on-street parking is limited (by the street corners and the turning circle).
- There might be problems over sites with **irregular boundaries** or unusable acute corner areas. This could affect the number of dwellings you can get on the site.
- Sometimes council might want to space MDH developments apart, separated by other housing styles, to prevent a sameness overtaking the **streetscape**.
- They don't like a row of **garages** across the front.
- Dwellings are not to have their main front doors positioned directly **opposite** each other.
- They don't want 'gun barrel' or 'barracks' development which creates '**bulky, monotonous and unbroken building layouts**' (in the words of one council control plan).
- Landscaping rules are very specific for MDH developments, requiring **screening** plantings both from the street and from neighbours, particularly for bedrooms and around driveways. You may have to install a reticulated **sprinkler** system (to encourage maintenance), path **lighting** and **signage** of a style which is not easily stolen or destroyed.
- Dwellings may require **private courtyards or lawn areas**—and these should have a **northerly orientation**. Council will not be pleased if they face the west or south.
- There may be a requirement in larger developments (e.g. six or more dwellings) that you create a **common open space area for**

outdoor entertaining, perhaps with barbecue facilities and, in the situation where the dwellings have at least two bedrooms, children's play equipment. Watch for these matters when planning your budget.
- You might have to design with **wheelchair access** in mind.

There are many more parameters than these, but they illustrate how councils now see the development of medium-density housing. Indeed, the council guide might describe a particular design issue using language like: 'This will be strongly discouraged'.

One of the more interesting concepts turning up in these documents is an assessment of how the style of your project fits in with the needs and requirements of the local market. Council may offer to provide demographic information to assist you in your design—choice of building materials and finishes, number and size of bedrooms, car parking provision and so on. This is a move beyond mere 'good design' as an end in itself and into the realm of neighbourhood or precinct fostering. It is also very difficult to pin down what this means in terms of concrete and glass.

As part of this trend, I have noticed some jadedness at council level with multi-unit developments which take fairly basic designs and try to give them style by tacking on a few bits of 'heritage' timber fretwork or by placing a couple of pots of cumquats by the front door for a Tuscan look.

Quiz your architect or designer to see if they have come to grips with council's design guidelines. You will soon ascertain whether they have understood the local bureaucratic mood of the moment or whether they are hoping simply to recycle a design scheme they have used elsewhere.

Putting it simply, it is in our interests not just to know these things so we can design our project without upsetting council, but to see if we can capture what councillors and their officers would love to see happen on the site. Then we will have many allies.

✓ *Tip:* Councils offer pre-lodgment meetings for developers to sort out problems before they occur. Take advantage of this procedure not simply to get the technical matters right, but to garner support from council officers.

What does the surveyor do?

A surveyor prepares a plan of the site showing boundaries and the distances between buildings (and other improvements such as a pool) and the boundaries. The surveyor's report confirms who owns the land and that it is fully contained (or not) within the legal title to that land. In other words, the report will warn you that you are about to construct three townhouses partly on the neighbour's block. The surveyor's plan will set out the subdivision.

It is a vital step to *link* what everyone thinks is going to happen—as they walk over the site—with ownership of the land and council requirements for alignments and setbacks.

If you don't know a surveyor, you should contact one of their professional associations for a referral. Take a look at www.surveying.org.au, which is the site of the Association of Consulting Surveyors Australia (ACSA). From there you can go to state and territory associations.

Sizing up a site for medium-density development

When inspecting a property for a medium-density project, think in terms of the potential for development. Check zoning and council local plans to see what is possible first.

Table 4.2 Development potential: medium density

Opportunity	Potential for development
Vacant land or house on large block	Room for additional dwellings
House with very wide side driveway—or the potential to create one	Vehicle access to new dwellings at rear of block
Big backyard *or* front yard	Room for additional dwellings at back or front of site
Site which is already multiple-density but which has been poorly executed	Site already has approval—a big plus; it can be redesigned by an architect to make valuable improvements or a more fashionable development

Table 4.2 continued

Opportunity	Potential for development
Room for driveway on each side of existing house	• Traffic flow is a serious issue for medium-density developments—cars must enter and exit property in a forwards direction • Assess site for separate vehicle entrance and exit or room for a turning circle
Wide frontage to road or corner position	• Allows more than one dwelling to have road frontage and direct vehicle access • Can create private yards in front of these dwellings rather than behind
Sloping site	Allows some car parking to be provided beneath dwellings while retaining level foot access
North-facing site	• Very desirable feature for individual courtyards or garden spaces • Can dwellings be positioned to take advantage of northerly orientation and to avoid or shelter from westerly aspect?

Summary

- As part of urban consolidation, pressure remains on councils to create areas where medium-density housing projects are encouraged.
- Council may have specific documents to guide investors with medium-density housing projects—get hold of a copy.
- Discuss council's guidelines with your architect/designer and surveyor.
- Arrange a pre-lodgment meeting with council officers to discuss your proposal in greater depth.

5

Changing the permitted use

Property does not exist independently of the world around it—it sits within a local council zoning scheme of some kind or other. The scheme permits the property to be used for certain things and might also specifically mention a number of uses which are unacceptable.

Within this scheme, however, there is room for the active property investor to work the margins. You can apply to council (or, in some cases, the state authority) to have the zoning changed for one or more properties or to have a change of use approved for your site. In general terms, it is possible to value-add to a property by changing its current use into one which is more profitable. At the most simplistic level, a residential zoning is more valuable than a rural zoning, and a commercial or industrial zoning might be worth more than a residential one. In particular locations or at different times, the reverse might also be true.

The investor makes money here by getting a profitable change of use or zoning approved by council. The great benefit—particularly for the inexperienced—is that the process should be cheaper than if you were seeking, for example, approval for a specific development such as a set of townhouses. In fact, you don't need to have anything specific prepared or even in mind at the time you apply—you might just be looking for consent for a general shift of permitted use from residential to commercial. And once you've got your consent, the property should immediately be more valuable—if you have provided what the market wants.

Table 5.1 Development by 'change of use'

Advantages	Disadvantages
The cost is relatively low—it is an intellectual exercise of paperwork and persuasion.	Unless you have a pre-arranged tenant or purchaser for the property, you are proceeding on the assumption you will have a market for the property with its new approved use or zoning.
You don't have to build anything.	A rezoning or change of use application is a threat to neighbours—no one can predict what will happen under the new arrangement. You can expect objections unless your application actually cures a localised anomaly and brings it in line with the prevailing use or zoning.
You can improve the value of your property by gaining council approval for a wider variety of permitted uses.	The costs of owning the property might increase. Find out about council and water rates, council contributions (which you have to pay), any applicable licensing requirements and insurance premiums.
You can negotiate to have the contract for your purchase of the property made conditional upon the issue of council approval for the change of use or rezoning. If you don't get the approval, you can back out of the purchase.	

'Change of use' strategies

What sorts of 'change of use' are worth seeking for your site? Here are some examples which have been used successfully by investors.

Kids' stuff

It was a real eye opener when I first heard of an investor whose tactic was to purchase ordinary, large homes and convert their use from residential to 'childcare facility' (that is, a kindergarten or childcare centre). 'The rent you'll get is significantly higher than for a home,' he said, 'and you've got most of the essentials on hand, including a kitchen, multiple rooms, a good yard, outdoor shedding and storage, and plumbing running down one side of the property (for laundry and bathroom) which can be developed to provide children's toilets and basins.'

Boarding

Many old pubs and large Victorian terrace houses have successfully been converted to backpacker lodgings. Budget tourism is now a large section of the market, with a customer base motivated strongly by a desire to pay as little as possible for accommodation so they can stay longer. Fire and safety requirements can add significantly to the development costs, but the ongoing revenue stream from this type of project is very desirable.

Tourism and education

Tourism is an unruly thing. Councils try to plan for it, but it has a funny habit of venturing off in unexpected directions—or of failing to take off at all. Some of the most intense investors target properties which have tourism zoning because they might be able to take advantage of development controls which can be more generous in some ways (while remaining restrictive in other ways) than typical commercial and residential controls. If the desired tourism operators don't start building, there can be opportunities for others with slightly different aims. Similarly, zonings for 'education' purposes are sometimes twisted if the council finds that developers are not beating a path to their door.

You need only look around your own area and read the local newspapers to see how yesterday's inspired plan can become today's failed town planning exercise. When dreams fall apart, the prepared property investor steps in and picks up a bargain. Get hold of copies of zoning instruments and maps and take a look at permitted and prohibited uses from one zoning to another: this can alert you to opportunities.

Retirement housing

New South Wales pioneered a scheme in the 1980s to encourage developers to construct retirement residential complexes. This was achieved by use of a tasty carrot: you could put more homes on to a site if their occupation was restricted to people over the age of 55 than if they were available to the general community. State Environmental Planning Policy Number 5 (SEPP 5, as it is called) has had a controversial life as it overrides the zoning and planning powers of council in order to meet its objectives. Developers have targeted areas using SEPP 5 as their shoehorn. While many would say this has been a poor planning move, others point out that retirement housing is an expensive and difficult area of work and developers needed a strong incentive if they were to take up the challenge.

✓ *Tip:* From time to time, state governments and local councils actually want private developers to create something specific and will encourage this type of development. Find out what's on your council's wish list at the moment.

Residential to commercial

Got an historic house located near the shops? This could become an office instead of someone's home. Generally speaking, the same property with a commercial use and rent will earn you more than with a residential use and rent. This could be a doubling of your cashflow when you add all the benefits together.

- A tenant generally pays higher rent for commercial as opposed to residential property.
- This means the property, now commercial, should be worth more to sell.
- A commercial tenant typically pays the property outgoings (water rates, council rates), or a share thereof.
- A commercial tenant may wish to refurbish the property at their own cost or at shared cost.
- As landlord of a commercial property you will register for GST, add GST to the rent but also get the GST back on your related expenses (this does not happen with ordinary residential property ownership).

You know the sorts of properties which successfully make the move to a commercial use. It might be the heritage house (or apartment block) with large rooms, high ceilings and ornate timberwork on the windows, doors and architraves. It could be the old residence above the shop. They tend to have the following things in common:

- **Proximity to an existing commercial shopping centre**. The property does not have to front the main shopping street—it can be down a side street but it must be near the retail strip. Sometimes a slight amount of distancing is a genuine advantage: it makes the property close enough to the action without the noise, pollution and anti-social behaviour of the main drag.
- **Lower rent**. This is where the newcomer will find a first spot to launch their business in the area. Yes, the tenant might move on when the business becomes established and successful. But if the shopping centre is thriving there will be an ongoing flow of new businesses looking for a similar, affordable entrance-level opportunity.
- **Parking**. Many traditional offices in local shopping centres offer no parking, either for customers or for the business owners. This is a major drawback for professionals like doctors, lawyers, accountants and estate agents, who may be on the move quite a bit during the day. The beauty of many residential properties adjacent to local shops is that there should be a parking spot for the boss at least—and he or she doesn't have to delve into the bowels of a multiplex carpark just to make a quick trip in the car. This is an advantage to look for when buying or developing this type of property. How can you create parking spots? If the property is a house, it may be possible to incorporate customer parking in the former back or front yard. Others do it by pushing a car space into a front bedroom of the old house/apartment. Whatever way you do it, car parking can add substantial value and appeal to a property with a commercial use.

A hook to hang your hat on

From his desk on the 23rd floor of a fashionable office block in the heart of Sydney, Dylan gazed out the window and enjoyed the expansive views. He was on the phone to one of his investor friends and they were discussing the possibility of doing a development with a group of two or three similarly minded, cashed-up professionals. They weren't sure what they would do—what sort of project it might be—they just knew they wanted to do more than simply own property passively and wait for the capital gain to emerge.

Not long afterwards, an opportunity appeared. There was a retail shopping strip lining one of the major roads out of the city. It had been retail for at least a hundred years with almost no major development. As such, it now had an historical and raffish charm and had remained profitable for the businesses along the route.

In the midst of all these shops were a number of residential terrace houses. Most of their neighbours had long since been converted to shops but a handful remained as homes, hemmed in by the commercial demands on all sides.

The past had caught up with the present here—and this meant that it was almost impossible to get approval to demolish one of these treasured pieces of architecture. So these terrace houses just sat there, occupied by families who left them empty by day and who ate dinner in front of the TV at night. Dylan and his partners thought they could do something about this. They sniffed a profit.

Acting in a cavalier fashion, they pooled their resources and bought one of these terraces with a vague plan to convert its approved use from residential to commercial. Surprisingly, they had carried out no effective research before committing to the purchase. However, once contracts *had* been exchanged, Dylan raced down to council to see what he could uncover.

'Clearly this property was now an anomaly,' said Dylan, 'surrounded as it was by commercial properties. I knew if I dug hard enough I would find a justification for council to convert the property to commercial. There *had* to be something there, something we could hang our hat on.'

Sure enough, after ploughing through council's files on the property, Dylan found his hook. 'Back in the 1930s there had been some sort of commercial use of the property. It was not absolutely clear what the details were, but there was a sniff of something commercial. Even though this was so long ago, council was prepared to accept this as a rationale for a change of use from residential to commercial.

'The area was now quite up-market and I felt sure that council officers had to put up with a lot of pushy idiots and tough developers giving them a hard time as they went about their job. I decided to play it differently—after all, we needed the council officers to be on our side, to respond to the logic of a change of use for our terrace.

'So I would change out of my business suit and dress casually before I left my office on the way to visit council. I threw myself upon their good graces, saying I was really just an ordinary bloke who needed a break. I wanted to enlist them as friends, not opponents. And they responded extremely well to this more humble and respectful approach, granting development consent for non-specific commercial use.

'Now we had to sell the thing,' said Dylan. 'We weren't sure who would use the property for their shop, so we just did the basics to the shell of the building. We cleaned it up, fixed minor problems, knocked down an internal wall, put in a shopfront window and door, sanded the timber floors and painted the walls white. We wanted to create a "canvas" on which an entrepreneur could visualise their own business. Fortunately the property sold quickly and we were in the clear with a good profit to show for our efforts.'

Reflecting on the deal, Dylan had this to say: 'We were maybe a bit foolish in purchasing the property before we knew we could get the change of use through council. But the place was such an anachronism—logic dictated that it had to turn commercial at some point. And as for council officers, they were concerned about creating a precedent that would set off a chain of loose-cannon developers. They just needed one hook which would give them the necessary excuse to treat this terrace house as a special case.'

Council zoning and planning documents generally allow some degree of evidence of prior use to justify a change. However, you can expect to find limits on how far back you can go; prior use rights can be lost. Dylan and his partners were fortunate indeed that council officers let them go back to the 1930s. Really, they were open to the change of use for a range of other town planning reasons as well—for example, simply to tidy up the commercial strip along the main road.

✓ *Tip:* Ask yourself why no one has applied for a change of use before. Are you missing some vital piece of information?

Principles for pursuing a 'change of use' application

If you are assessing a property for its potential after a change of permitted use or zoning, consider the following:

- Go to council before you purchase. Know the local zoning and permitted uses.
- Don't rely on what you see on the street—council's view of the area and its future may have changed since other developments were approved.
- Inspect council's file on the specific property. See if there are any hooks from which you can hang your change of use proposal.
- If you plan to rely on a prior or existing use ensure you get council officers to *show you*, by reference to the documents, why you ought to be able to do what you want to do with the property and its future use. If *they* can't justify your desired use of the property, you might well find it even more difficult to persuade them of the same thing.
- Look for the *compelling logic* behind the change of use you propose.
- You may wish to engage an expert town planning consultant to assist with your application. Council will provide you with the necessary forms, but you will have to prepare supporting documentation and it is here that the town planning consultant can ensure you produce evidence for the relevant criteria. In some situations and zonings, it might be necessary to apply to the state authority for consent.
- Unless you know precisely what type of business will tenant or purchase the completed property from you, get your consents for permitted use in general, non-specific terms.
- Liaise with local estate agents and business brokers so that you have an idea about any necessary or desirable building improvements, facilities and decoration. 'Change of use' is a marketing issue: who will your customers be?
- Find out about any heritage listings if you are checking out an old, classic or popular building or landscape. If there is a local residents' action group you would not be wasting your time by finding out if there would be community opposition to your plan.
- Check that the current use for the property is in fact an approved use—the owner or tenant might be operating in breach of the rules and without council consent.
- Have a back-up plan for the property in case something goes wrong: see Chapter 11.

Sizing up a property for a change of permitted use

When inspecting a piece of land for a 'change of use' application, think in terms of the potential for development (see Table 5.2).

Table 5.2 Potential for development: change of use

Opportunity	Potential for development
Residential premises abutting or in the middle of a shopping strip or industrial zone	A more valuable: • commercial use, or • industrial use
Pub or old-fashioned guest house	Backpacker lodgings
A failed council local plan or development (e.g. tourism precinct, industrial estate, education zone)	Change of use or zoning may be favourably considered where previously it would not have been entertained
Dying industrial zone	Change to residential or commercial (e.g. entertainment)
Rural land at urban fringe	• Residential housing estate • Shopping centre

Summary

- You can develop a property by changing its authorised use: residential, commercial, industrial, tourism, entertainment, education and many others.
- Council may have its own reasons for wanting to support your application for a change of use—see if you can align with council's desires for that area or for specific property.
- Look for properties which are out of harmony with their neighbours.
- 'Change of use' is a marketing issue too. Who will your purchaser or tenant be?
- Understand what the local zoning and planning instruments have to say about prior use rights.

6

Subdivision: Drawing new lines on the land

As our suburbs and towns continue their urban sprawl, there is an ongoing need for more homesites. It starts when farms get chopped into hobby farms, then into 2 hectare blocks or small blocks for new suburbs. And the lots are getting smaller.

Most of us who've grown up in Australia were raised in urban environments. Are we ready to launch into green fields subdivision? Or should we stick with urban properties and cram more lots into the existing space? In Chapter 4 we looked at the idea of subdividing the backyard of your home and putting in an extra lot or two. In this chapter we will consider land subdivision itself, without the construction element.

Pros and cons of land subdivision

Why buy vacant land for subdivision instead of buying a house or strata unit as your investment vehicle? There are many arguments both for and against (see Table 6.1).

Table 6.1 Vacant land subdivision

Arguments for	Arguments against
You are not stuck trying to work with an outdated design—for buildings or land subdivision. It's a blank slate.	There's no rental income from a tenant to offset against the mortgage over the lengthy period from land acquisition to sale of the new lots. However, some sites (if fenced and large enough) are suitable for agistment. Contact a rural or stock and station agent.
You don't have to engage builders, with all the uncertainty and risk this involves.	If you are earning no income from the site, there may be difficulty claiming tax deductions. There are issues of expenditure against income and expenditure of a capital nature. Ensure you get expert advice.
You don't have to worry about tenants vandalising a dwelling, the costs of advertising for tenants or the fees of a managing agent.	You might have to pay for roadworks or for more extensive roadworks than you initially budgeted for; this can be very expensive.
You don't have to worry about the hidden costs of unexpected excavation or foundations—they become the purchasers' problem.	Costs for connecting to services—electricity, telephone, sewer, water, gas—are expensive (but should be ascertainable in advance).
Although it is expensive to connect services to vacant land, your financial exposure is less *per lot* than if you were to erect a dwelling on each lot.	You need to monitor the site regularly, as there are ongoing maintenance issues over a lengthy period. These could involve slashing grass, weed control, fencing and rubbish clearance (people might dump their trash and old cars there). Maintenance involves minimising bushfire risk—it is a serious business on the urban fringe.
If you decide to move to construction, you get more value for your money when building a new dwelling than when modifying or redesigning an existing one.	The land area might be large enough for a profitable number of lots, but there can be substantial areas of 'waste', such as sharply sloping land, watercourses, easements for drainage or right of way, trees protected by preservation order and setbacks from roads. These factors might affect the size or number of lots for the site—and the profitability.
	It can be difficult to find out in advance whether there will be major restrictions on where a house can be built on each lot—

Table 6.1 continued

Arguments for	Arguments against
	the building 'envelope'. Bushfire, flooding, watercourses, rights of way, etc., might restrict the number of allotments or render valueless certain desirable natural features of the site (views, proximity to natural bushland, privacy).
	Watch out for land tax liability.
	There can be unexpected problems over road access to the site. Before you purchase, find out which authority owns the adjacent road(s) and confirm you can get car access and where it can be positioned. Be wary of relying on what, for example, council officers might say if in fact the road is owned by a state authority. There are issues about cars slowing down to enter your subdivision, turning left/right, number of vehicles, position of entry and exit, signage, median strips and, ultimately, the route of any internal road and lot placement.

Roads and building envelopes

Stan was in manufacturing and ran his factory with something of an iron fist. When times became hard for his industry, he had to fight hard to survive.

In better times he had purchased a little weekender so he could grab some quality time with his family. It was a cottage out in the country, about an hour and a half from Sydney. And he owned pretty much the whole little valley it was in—around 20 hectares of pasture and woodlands.

As his income dried up, he looked around for things to sell. He realised he might have to get rid of the weekender. Speaking to a local real estate agent, he found out that several of the local 'city folk' were not just selling their holiday homes to like-minded blow-ins from the city, but were sub-dividing the properties into smaller allotments.

With the agent in tow, he could see the dollar signs in his own eyes. Yes, he could turn all that lazy bushland into profitable mini-farms. He could hang on to his weekender, with a small amount of land around it, and find the cash to save his business too.

So Stan launched into it. Got the surveyor out there, prepared some subdivision plans, got a rough idea from the local council about his chances of gaining approval and, most importantly, began marketing the properties. This was the part that the estate agent was particularly enthused by. Each block would be around 2–3 hectares in size, this being the minimum allotment allowed by the zoning in that location. There would be room for a house and a pony or trailbike.

The signs went up at the entrance to his valley. Pictures of rural bliss appeared in the estate agency window.

But the plans hit a giant snag in the form of council. All along he had known he would have to pay a number of expenses—things like wire fencing, the surveyor, the lawyer, the council fees. But he hadn't counted on the difficulty involved in getting approval for a house site on each lot of the subdivision.

Most of the valley was cleared pasture. Higher up on all sides the land became heavily wooded. And the land was undulating: picturesque but difficult to drive over. The council and the local bushfire authority were startled at the plan to locate houses high up, where they would get the best views. 'No, no, no,' they said. 'If there's a fire we won't be able to get our trucks up to protect the houses.'

The council specified a 'building envelope'—a single place to site a dwelling—for each allotment. Actually, there were some allotments where council would not approve a home site at all. This was the first frustration. It meant that some lots were of almost no saleable value—the owners could not build on them. Second, owners would not be able to build in the most attractive locations on the allotments. High, romantic vantage points with the best views were out.

Still, he thought, at least the purchasers will be able to erect homes on most allotments, even if not in the most desirable locations. But the council and fire authority were not finished with him and his plans. 'Roads, all-weather access' were the next words he heard. The current road along the floor of the valley, which would link all the allotments, was just a winding goat track. This would not support emergency vehicles or the potential traffic of so many owners. It would be a substantial, unbudgeted cost to upgrade nearly a kilometre of road and install associated drainage, one which would run into tens of thousands of dollars. Stan was tearing out his hair. And his creditors were banging at the door of his factory.

Meanwhile, the estate agent had successfully lined up a number of prospective purchasers. Each wanted their slice of the rural dream. But, without council approval, sale contracts were stalled. Council was sitting on the development, waiting until every question was answered to its satisfaction—quite properly, too, given the risk and danger to home owners and firefighters.

Eventually, some time and a couple of stomach ulcers later, the council issued its approval. There were quite a number of conditions placed on the approval, and the cost of meeting them would be considerable, but at least there was progress. Contracts were exchanged with several buyers and cash flowed in.

Subdivision checklist

When assessing a site for its suitability for subdivision run through the following checklist.

1 **Establish subdivision potential**. Contact council about these preliminary matters:
   - the current zoning for the site;
   - whether there are proposals to change that zoning or the zoning of nearby properties;
   - the potential number and minimum size of lots which can be created there;
   - whether a dwelling house can be constructed on each lot;
   - whether there has been a failed previous attempt to subdivide this property. If so, why did it fail?

2 **Establish potential value**. Speak to local real estate agents about:
   - selling prices for the lots;
   - what local buyers are looking for (size, shape, services, access, etc.);
   - what the competition is like;
   - timing—when should the lots be marketed for sale? After spring rain? Before summer's heat? When there is snow on the mountains nearby?

3. **Establish the nature and extent of the hurdles**. Speak to a town planning consultant (Chapter 7) and a surveyor about:
   - their experience with this council over subdivision;
   - what council is likely to require as conditions of consent;
   - the approximate cost per lot for services connection and other subdivision overheads;
   - limitations with this particular site which might affect the number and size of the lots;
   - how long it will take to get the lots to the point of sale.
4. **Establish your likely net profit**. Contact your accountant for information about how this 'profit' will actually look after taxation. There will be critical issues of timing, capital gains and tax deductibility.

These matters constitute the preliminaries. At this point, you should be in a position to know if the subdivision is an affordable investment and roughly what you will make from it if things go according to plan.

Get an expert guide

'It's one thing to be an experienced property investor,' said April, 'but quite another thing to actively subdivide a property. When you start out, it is vital to get it right, so don't be cheap. Hire an expert to guide you through the process.'

April purchased a green field that was ripe for subdivision. It was around 18 500 square metres in size but had only a narrow frontage to the road—about 30 metres. She was nervous about the project and decided to engage a town planning consultant. He recommended a three-lot subdivision that would give April large lifestyle blocks which would attract a premium price for the area. This would be better than cutting the main block into many smaller pieces of less-certain value.

'I had been thinking about cutting the large block into a number of battle-axe allotments, each with a narrow driveway snaking down to the main road,' said April. 'The consultant, however, persuaded me to push further into the block with my own larger roadway, creating a cul-de-sac off which all lots would gain access and wider frontages.

'I was a little reluctant to do this as it would involve the cost—and difficulty—of building a real road, not just a driveway. But his expertise gave me the confidence to do it. And he helped find the right road-builders to make it happen.

'So we put in the road, landscaping, fencing and services—I had to bring electricity, water and the sewer to all blocks. Two of the lots were almost 7000 square metres in size and the third was 4500 square metres. An estate agent has told me that the finished blocks will be worth between $220 000 and $230 000 each.'

Development costs were reasonably high—around $70 000 per allotment. If it had been a ten-lot subdivision the developer, in that location, could expect to shave around $10 000 off the cost per allotment. Here are the basic figures:

Gross sale value (estimate):		$660 000 to $690 000
Less		
Purchase price (land only)	$150 000	
Development costs	$210 000	
Sales agent's commission	$19 800	
Total costs	$379 800	$379 800
	profit (before tax)	**$280 200 to $310 200**

'I'll get most of my development costs back on the first allotment, profit from the second, and I might just keep the third. It was worth it to pay for a guide,' said April.

Filling in the details

Once you feel the subdivision has potential, it is time to fill in the details and move to a more accurate costing and sales projection. Generally, it's not too hard to come up with the basic plan. A surveyor will check with council requirements for allotment sizes, frontages and so on, then draw your plan of subdivision suitable for registration. Your solicitor, in consultation with the surveyor, will prepare other registration documents dealing with the creation of legal encumbrances which will affect the lots.

Legal encumbrances

These can include:

- internal **roads**;
- **rights of way**: access for people and vehicles over the site;
- **easements**: for surface water drainage and the positioning for services. These things have to go somewhere; they will limit the usability of various lots (where the owner can build);
- **covenants**: prescribing types of permitted and prohibited building materials, fencing and possibly use of the land. This is a traditional way of establishing a style for the subdivision which can impact favourably on future development and construction.

✓ *Tip:* Covenants can be used to support a marketing plan for a prestige development, where cheap building materials (corrugated iron sheds, weatherboard homes, wire or metal fences) are prohibited and positive design elements are incorporated across a wide area for the benefit of all owners in the subdivision (e.g. that there be no fences across the front of any lot).

Encumbrances are legal matters as well as issues for the surveyor. When it comes to discussions with council officers, a range of details must be clarified before the plans are prepared. These include:

- **Water**. If the land is sloping, there will be issues of run-off. If it is flat, what are the chances of flooding? Council should be able to tell you the flood risk for the property and whether this category of risk would affect building proposals. Council might also be able to tell you whether there are watercourses across the site or whether the act of building homes upon the land will introduce drainage issues. Council might require the legal creation on title of drainage easements as part of the subdivision. One of the most important consequences of the creation of such easements is that there might be building restrictions. This will affect the building envelope for the allotments.

- **Fire**. Increasingly, this is becoming a serious factor in the development of a subdivision in a bushland setting. Don't be caught by surprise on this one. Everyone gets the shakes after a bad experience with bushfire—like the rebuilding of 400 homes following the Canberra fires in the summer of 2003. Look wider than just council—even insurance companies are moving towards a policy of declining to insure certain vulnerable homes. This could hammer your sales marketing. If planning a subdivision in an area faced with a bushfire risk, you might wish to consider consulting about fire issues with a wider range of people than just your surveyor, estate agent, lawyer, accountant and council officers. For example, can you line up a willing insurer for your buyers' homes?
- **Views and privacy**. If the subdivision site is level and suburban, the issues of privacy and views are much more straightforward than if the site (or part thereof) is elevated, sloping or open to views on one or more sides. You can stave off nasty fighting and give your marketing a boost by having an architect involved in settling the boundaries between allotments. Would some landscaping—such as the planting of advanced trees—help satisfy the concerns for privacy among potential purchasers? Much good work can be achieved by angling the building envelopes to maximise views and/or privacy.
- **Contributions to council**. Roads are only one area where council might want a contribution from the subdivision developer. Others may include space for recreation, buffer zones, roundabouts, parking—find out from council what sorts of things they are keen to collect on (see chapter 10).
- **Environmental and heritage concerns**. The developer should always ask about these issues, even where the land to be subdivided is pretty much barren earth. Bats, birds, frogs—we've all heard stories of how these little creatures have derailed the plans of mighty developers. They can upset smaller developers too. Make the inquiries.

  Consider the heritage issues surrounding any human-constructed structures currently on the site. It is surprising what one person will consider rubbish while another wants it preserved for future generations. I recall a small timber structure—one room, really—lined with pictures that went back a hundred years. An absolute gem, it had been a meeting hall for a community organisation now long gone. It was a remarkable time capsule for its local town, though few people went inside. Outside, it was suffering from a lack of maintenance and looked like nothing other than an old wooden shed. Still, one day the local fire brigade decided it would burn it down as part of a practice drill. Only last-minute action by concerned locals helped save it.

You might think that home sites would not cut into Aboriginal sacred sites. However, this is not true. While this is most unlikely in the middle of the suburbs, it is something that must not be taken for granted in greenfield or bushland subdivisions. Recently the issue emerged for a young couple who had purchased a block in Alice Springs. Their plans were unexpectedly stalled when a sacred site was identified on the land. At the time of writing, the matter had not been finalised. Was there a sacred site? In any event, it was clearly difficult for everyone involved.

These are matters where respect is due. Yet they run headlong into the profit equation. Be mindful of the possibilities when assessing a site for development. Understand that these are often areas where considerable expertise is required to make a full assessment—don't expect to get that advice informally or from council officers in the absence of official investigation and reporting on the site.

The placement of a dwelling on land is not a simple matter. Council will have many rules and prohibitions affecting which way the front door and windows face, orientation of any private courtyards, the path taken by a long driveway, minimum road frontage for each lot, minimum depth of the lot, and so on. While these are matters for your experts, I must stress that you cannot leave the issue of placement entirely in their hands. It is prudent to understand the design limitations and to actively walk the site yourself with this in mind.

Working in unfamiliar territory

Almost by accident Helena came upon a potential subdivision site in the Dandenong Ranges outside Melbourne. Perhaps a chat with an estate agent one weekend put the idea into her head. And for many months she had been in the background, circling around a property and family in distress, tasting a deal but never biting. Finally the exhausted family members gave in and sold.

This was the deal: the old farm was around 14 hectares in size. Sitting on it was the original modest timber farmhouse and, in another corner, a derelict, never-completed dream home. The property had been owned by a businessman who went broke during the construction of his personal mansion. Once he took his hand off the project, some members of his family raided the place and ran off with everything that was moveable. They unscrewed the taps, the light switches, light fittings, doors and more; they punched holes in the walls; a ceiling was falling down due to lack of maintenance. It was a mess and very unattractive.

At a giveaway price, it had potential. Unlike other prospective buyers over the previous year, Helena didn't give a toss about the wreck. It didn't concern her at all—it was merely an issue to be allowed for in the figures.

Helena wanted to keep her cashflow under control, so her first step was to offload the old farmhouse. She went to council and inquired about subdivision. On the figures, she could get three lots of the minimum 4 hectares in size from the block. But, because the farmhouse had been there before the current planning instruments, the council would let her subdivide it off on a half-hectare block. 'It was a bonus extra block,' she said.

This she duly did—and recovered one-third of the purchase price for the total site. This kept the bank happy and gave her strong financial control over the site.

She knew it would take some time to get the necessary approvals and complete the subdivision, so her next step was to fix up the vandalised mansion and put in a tenant. This too assisted her cashflow position markedly.

Then things started to go wrong. It was not her part of the world, so she looked in the phone book and found a surveyor to prepare the subdivision plan and development application.

'I chose a local surveyor rather than one from the city because I knew the advantage of getting someone who was plugged into council, who would know all the right people,' said Helena. 'However, it turned out he was plugged into all the *wrong* people at council. They hated him. With hindsight I can see that my DA was doomed from the start. Gradually it became obvious from discussion when I attended meetings at council offices—they did not like my surveyor. They had it in for him.'

Unbelievably it took a year to overcome this self-imposed hurdle and to get the subdivision approved. One of the real stumbling blocks was that Helena was too busy in her full-time job to get out of the city and sort things out more quickly.

That was not to be the end of her troubles. She needed a whole range of contractors to put the services on to the new lots: power, water, phone, fencing; she had to put something like 200 metres of roadway through the front of the lots (and that alone was a $30 000 expense).

'I was ripped off everywhere I turned,' said Helena. 'They knew I wasn't a local and I was made to pay. For example, a contractor erected a power pole on my neighbour's property because it was an easier job than putting it where it was supposed to go—on one of my lots! I had to have the argument about removing it and doing the job again. Can you believe it?!

'What's more, I found there was no one who I could complain to about any of this slipshod and overpriced work—all the contractors knew each other or were related by birth or marriage. I had to keep my frustration to myself!'

Shape and access options

When assessing a potential site for subdivision you will generally have a number of options for how the plan will be laid out. Some of these options will get you into hot water with council, yet will seem quite reasonable to you. There is a lot of baggage in this process—including past unfortunate experiences which council officers regret and ever-evolving visions of what constitutes good town planning. It helps to get advice on layout from more than one expert.

The battle-axe

You can subdivide behind a row of houses or other properties if you can gain access for people and vehicles (see Figure 6.1). It could be vacant farm land behind a ribbon development along the road, or it could be a consolidation of a number of large backyards which you split off from their houses. Access—the handle of the battle-axe—does not have to be 'owned' by the new lots but can be delivered through a 'right of way' registered on the legal titles of the lands benefited and burdened by the right of way.

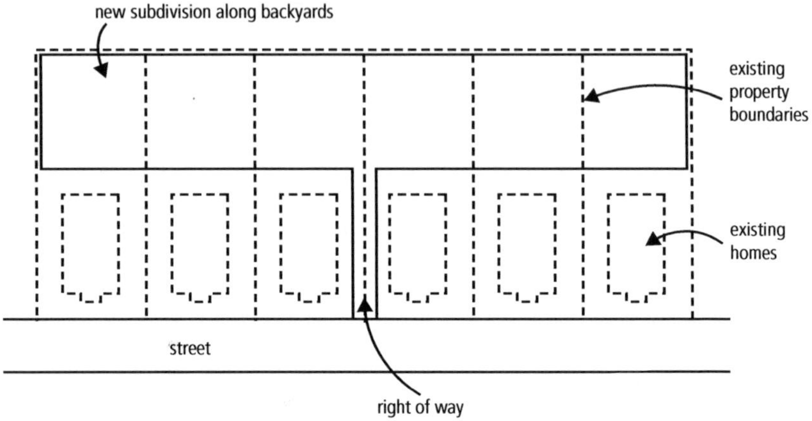

Figure 6.1 The battle-axe

The dormitory

While it might still be possible to design your subdivision in a strip like this (see Figure 6.2), real estate agents will advise against it. They find that purchasers simply do not like this style of subdivision any more.

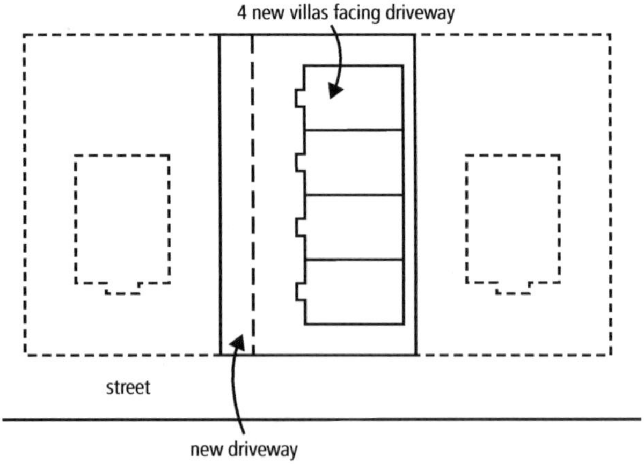

Figure 6.2 The dormitory

Face-to-face versus angled

There is a simple way to put new homes on your site—but councils don't like it. They do not want front doors and key windows staring straight into one another (see Figure 6.3). They prefer these features to be screened or set at an angle (see Figure 6.4).

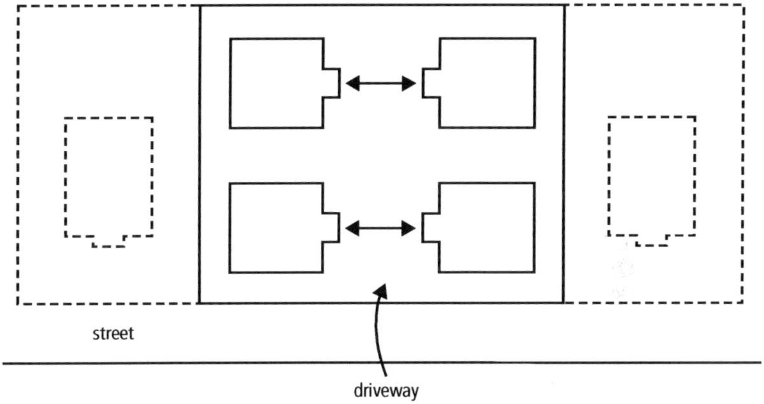

Figure 6.3 Face-to-face

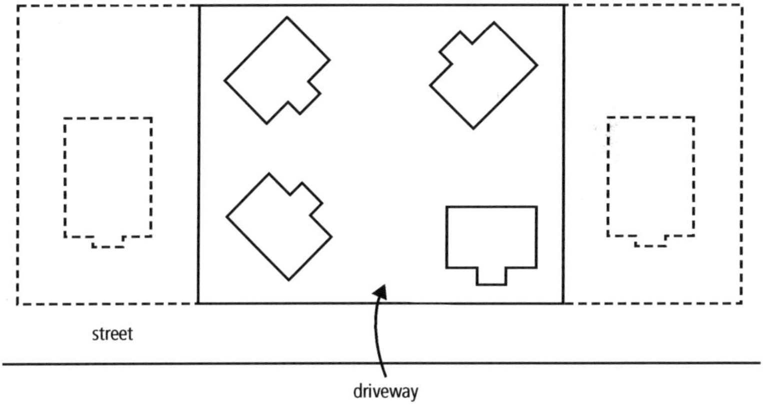

Figure 6.4 Angled features

Off-the-grid

A popular solution is to scatter the dwellings across the site rather than position them on a rigid grid of right angles (see Figure 6.5). A winding road and clever use of landscaping can bring a village or community feel to the development.

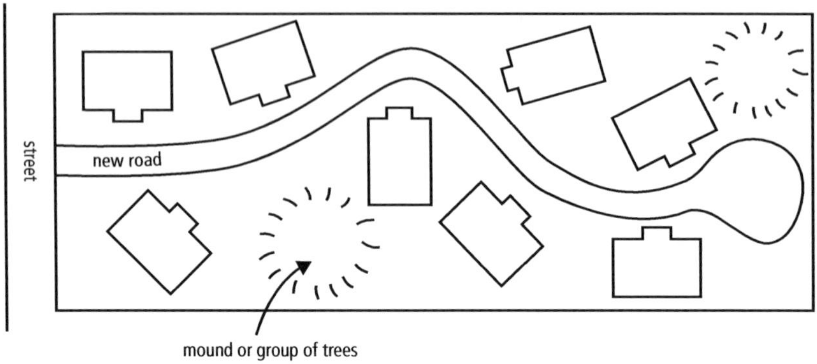

Figure 6.5 Off-the-grid

Terrace houses

Councils don't seem to mind rows of terrace houses where they look out to good views or across wide expanses of parkland (see Figure 6.6). A heritage architectural theme also seems to help.

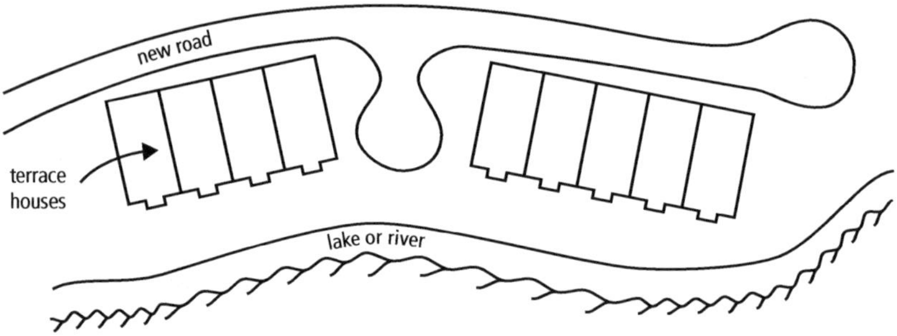

Figure 6.6 Terrace houses

Road or driveway?

There are two ways of providing access to a battle-axe block. You can bring the road up to where the subdivision starts and give each lot a driveway on to the narrow opening (see Figure 6.7) or, more desirably, push the road further into the subdivision and create a turning circle where each lot has a direct and more spacious connection to the common road (see Figure 6.8). The second alternative will cost the developer more space and additional road construction expense, but creates more valuable lots.

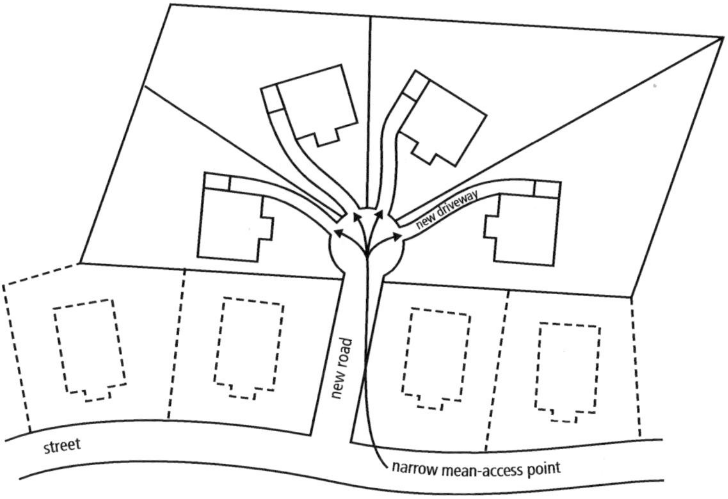

Figure 6.7 Many driveways

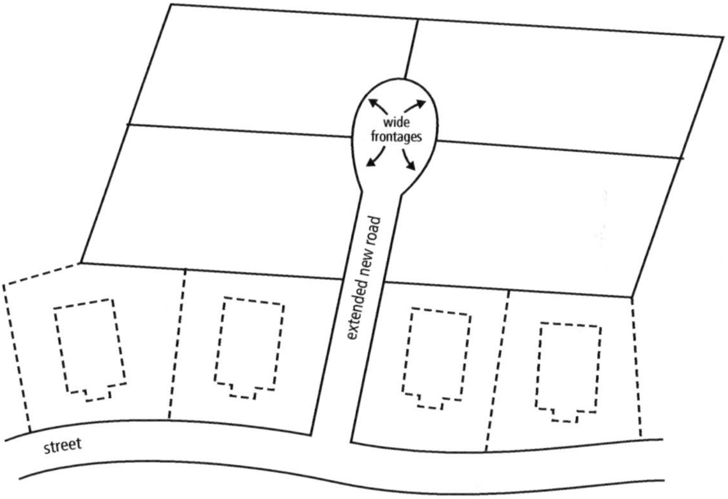

Figure 6.8 Common road

The best layout for your subdivision will emerge after seeking advice from a number of experts: your surveyor, town planning consultant, architect, assorted engineers (if required), council officers and the estate agent charged with the marketing and sale of the properties. But you are at the helm of this team. Walk the site and see how various possible designs for dwellings and for access will work in different ways on the same piece of land.

Playing by the numbers

Is numerology a sound basis for property development? It seemed to work for Stefan, who believes certain numbers are critical for success while others guarantee trouble.

'There was a new subdivision on a low rise on the edge of a prestigious part of the city,' said Stefan. 'The whole tone of the subdivision conveyed the impression of quality. The blocks were large and most had excellent views to the hills. It was the sort of place where you could spread out and build your ultimate home. But the cost of the blocks was high.

'There was a lot of interest in the subdivision and, even though I wasn't ready to build, I knew—because of the location, the high entry price and the quality feel—that I should take a gamble and secure one of the blocks for future purposes. Maybe I would build a home there, maybe not.

'At that early stage there weren't even roads on the ground—just a plan. I jumped in and purchased one of the largest blocks, which was around 1800 square metres in size. It cost me $80 000. Most of the site was useable, but some parts sloped away significantly. I completed the purchase and just sat on it, doing nothing and biding my time until I had a plan for it.

'The one thing I dreaded was getting allocated a "bad" street number. This was important to me. Sure enough, when they dealt out the street numbers, my block got number 4. This was very bad news indeed. I just *hate* number 4—it stands for "death" in Chinese. Not a good omen. I was certainly not going to build my home and live there under that number.

'So I took a good look at what I had. The large block held the key. In our council area, the minimum size for an allotment was 600 square metres. I realised I could possibly get away with subdividing my lot into three lots of 600 square metres each. Bear in mind that at this stage not all lots in the original subdivision had been sold or built upon. It would be audacious to subdivide my lot now—but it had to be done.

'Upon further thought and consultation, I scrapped one of the lots and decided to go with a two-lot subdivision, each lot measuring around 900 square metres. Parts of one of the blocks were just a little too steep to make a good homesite, and I knew there was greater value for me in maintaining the overall quality nature of the development.

'I was also thinking that with two lots I could number them 4a and 4b—a total of 8. This would bring about a dramatic turnaround in fortune! The number 8 is a "whole" number, a number that has no end to it—a favoured number.

'As my subdivision went ahead, I saw that fortune was indeed smiling upon me. Property prices in the suburb were increasing and demand for building blocks was high. When the subdivision was complete, I sold the top block for $150 000. And I kept the bottom block for myself.'

Why didn't the original subdivider do this? Stefan had this theory: 'At the time of the main subdivision, the developer believed that purchasers were looking for large blocks to take mansion-sized homes. He thought this was what would appeal to top-end customers. And he was probably right. But in the two years between commencement of his subdivision and when I did mine, the market had shifted. Demand for any decent home block had peaked. People could borrow more freely and the site had established more of a reputation as a quality location once the first homes were constructed.'

Sizing up a subdivision site

When inspecting a piece of land for subdivision, think in terms of the potential for development (see Table 6.2).

Table 6.2 Potential for development: subdivision

Opportunity	Potential for development
Close to services	These come at substantial cost so there are great savings to be made if power, gas, telephone, water and sewerage connections are at hand
Views	Check whether views can be maintained from all blocks after construction of homes
Flat	Flat means cheaper construction costs; check the site carefully for natural watercourses; understand how groundwater moves across the site as this may limit development
Undulating site	The site can be developed to maximise privacy between dwellings

Table 6.2 continued

Across from bushland	• Can the subdivision layout be designed to make it easier to protect homes from bushfires? • Seek information about design elements—for the site and for buildings—which will promote safety—for example, good all-weather vehicle access to the front and back of each lot; covenants on the title about building materials and designs
Corner position	Could minimise expense on constructing new internal roadways
Fencing	Is there current fencing which can be retained?
Dams can be constructed on each lot	• Water is a priority on any semi-rural 'acreage', such as subdivision into 2 hectare lots • Check that council will permit dam construction on each lot • This is an issue even where reticulated water service will be provided; large allotments need a number of water options

Summary

- When assessing a piece of land for potential subdivision, speak to the local council town planners then find a surveyor with significant subdivision experience in that council area.
- Be alert: a subdivision offers significant income to a whole host of consultants. Watch out for signs of self-interest clouding their judgement.
- Don't rely on information provided informally by council officers before the subdivision plans have been assessed by them.
- Areas of particular concern requiring your early attention include: building envelopes—size and location of house or building sites; roads and access; fire issues; kerbing and gutters; drainage—including water run-off; fencing; power and services—electricity, water, phone, gas; landscaping; environmental concerns—habitats, endangered species, special trees, etc.; parking and access to parking; contributions to council for matters such as recreation and parking; privacy and views.

- Where possible, check key measurements yourself. Your experts can sometimes get these things wrong—with serious consequences all round.
- Different experts will have varying opinions on the optimum layout for your subdivision. Get a range of views.
- If the subdivision is for larger semi-rural blocks, ensure that water is available and affordable.

Section II

WORKING WITH YOUR EXPERTS AND THE COUNCIL

7

Seeking council approval

Each state and territory has its own planning laws and regulations and each local council follows its own procedures for assessing applications and granting consents. It can become confusing. Who do you speak to? Which is the body charged with the power to issue a consent or approval? Most of this can be sorted out at your first visit to council offices. But there are subtleties to the process.

One trap is to assume that the rules and terminology in a new area will be the same as those in a suburb or state/territory with which you are familiar. Second, the investor should know how to handle the objections process. Third, understanding the role and usefulness of a town planning consultant as your expert guide is crucial. And finally, you need to know how to avoid designing your way into trouble with council officers and policies.

Know the terminology

Development consent

Demolition, construction, subdivision and change of use are examples of applications which must be approved by council. Typically this involves preparing and lodging with council one or more **development applications (DAs)**. Council is the **consent authority** and the developer is looking to obtain a **development consent** from council. However, it is not always the same process in each state and territory. In the Northern Territory, you approach a body called the Development Consent Authority (DCA)—council puts its own comments to the DCA about your application. In Victoria, you lodge a **planning application**, not a DA. In the ACT, you take your development application to a government agency called PALM (Planning and Land Management).

Building or construction consent

New construction requires its own approval by the relevant authority. In most states you prepare and lodge a separate **building application (BA)** for approval by the council. However, in New South Wales you apply for a **construction certificate**, which can come from council or an accredited private certifier. Council will give you a list of these. The ACT, the Northern Territory, Queensland and South Australia also use private certifiers to handle building applications and issue construction approvals. In Tasmania you can apply for all your consents at once—the whole process gets a single application number, rather than separate applications being required for each stage from demolition to subdivision to construction. For small jobs, it is sometimes the case that the two stages become one.

You should be aware that there have been some serious problems involving private certifiers. People talk about council officers and the potential for corruption (leading to approval or rejection of an application), but private certifiers work with the question mark of 'conflict of interests' hanging over them. At the end of the day, they are private businesses aiming to make a profit. If a developer squeezes them hard enough, the result may be that corners are cut—which won't show up until the development is built and sold off.

Some local councils have concerns about the use of private certifiers and may investigate your plans and approvals to see that everything has been done by the book. One area of particular focus which has been mentioned to me is where certifiers have not checked that construction plans accord with the conditions council placed on approval. For example, council might require, by way of condition, that a particular window or doorway be moved or angled differently. To avoid later expense and delay, the investor should go through the conditions to check that the amendments duly made it on to the construction plans before the construction certificate was issued.

Subdivision

In most places, the division of a piece of land into smaller parcels is called subdivision. However, the term **land division** is also in use, particularly in South Australia. This might be handled as a third application to council.

Handling objections

Investors must prepare their plans with a view to answering objections from the community—including those emanating from commercial rivals. How successful are objectors? Here, by way of example, are the figures for the 2001–02 financial year from the Victorian Civil and Administrative Tribunal (which handles appeals from the planning decisions of local councils in that state). These show that, in 9.5 per cent of applications, the objector was successful, while 43 per cent of appeals lodged by developers were successful in overturning a council decision.

A further 15 per cent of developer appeals were 'successful' to the extent that a compromise decision was reached. And 36 per cent of objectors were party to a compromise solution.

Flexibility is the key to survival, whether you are the investor or an objector. You can't always get *everything* you want . . . but you can mostly salvage the deal. And objectors can force some kind of useful compromise even if the thing they detest goes ahead in some shape or form. Their effort has not been wasted.

Councils have rules for alerting neighbours to a planned development, but there may also be a degree of discretion, both as to whom is advised and how long they have to object. A period of fourteen days (or ten 'business days')—running generally, but unhelpfully for objectors, from the date of council's letter not the date of posting or receipt by the addressee—is common for most simple developments, such as the erection or alteration of a dwelling. But don't take this for granted. If there are heritage or other issues which might complicate the matter you can expect council to provide a longer period for objectors to view the plans and lodge an objection. This might only be a further seven days—don't imagine it will stretch on forever.

Councils are increasingly sensitive to objectors and will often bend over backwards to let them get their gripes on to the record. But only to the point where council—that is, the elected councillors, not the staff—have issued an approval for the development. It may be possible to sneak in an objection right up until this defining point. Therefore it is in your interests not to leave the gate open longer than the bare minimum. For example, if you have failed to include key matters in your application, council could defer its decision. While this is the sort of thing that should be picked up much earlier by council officers, you also need to be sure you have complied with all requirements. If an objector leans hard enough on councillors, they will look for a way to stall your development and to provide time for the community to build its case against it.

Who gets notified?

Around the nation you will find different rules as to notification and advertising of a development. Adelaide Council, for example, has a policy of sending a letter to owners within 60 metres of the site under consideration, as well as to local interest groups and heritage societies if it considers them relevant. Perth's planning scheme prescribes who is to be notified according to the particular case. In New South Wales, it might just be adjoining neighbours who get a council letter about what you're doing. Signs are often stuck up at development sites to notify local residents.

Notification takes the form of a letter from council, sometimes with a plan of the proposed development attached if building work is to take place. The plan is not comprehensive, but will show the height of the building work and its location on the site relative to boundaries. It details the externals—shape, size, location—but not necessarily what's going on inside. You will be invited to check the full plans and application at council offices and given a date by which to lodge any submission or objection.

Clearly the smart developer finds out the rules and works out in advance who is going to get a letter from council. A pre-emptive visit to a neighbour or local interest group might be in order before they get the letter or read the address in council's usual block advert in the local newspaper.

Defence tactics: Making your own objection

Imagine you've purchased a modest single-storey cottage and intend, at some future date, to build an upstairs extension to take advantage of the ocean views—a great development idea. Then, out of the blue, you wake to the sound of builders unloading their gear from five vans two doors away. You run out in your pyjamas and all is revealed: a neighbour is putting up a top-floor extension starting today. Now he/she is going to get the views and block any from your property.

Defending your property interests is as much a part of active property investment as preparing a DA and engaging a builder. All developers should know how the objections process works in their council area.

Go to council's offices. Ask to see the register or listing of development consents and check these five things with counter staff:

- Was approval required for the work?
- If approval has not yet been granted, by what date and time must your objection be lodged?
- Who else got notified by council? (Work out who your allies might be.)
- If approval has been issued, when did this happen?
- Did the approval come from council or from some other authority?

At the same time, obtain copies of these documents:

- If already approved, the consent and the conditions attached;
- In any event, the relevant local zoning plan and the control plan which outlines the parameters for development.

Ask to speak to a council town planner—you might have to make an appointment and come back later. Inquire about these things:

- What precisely has been approved?
- Does the proposed development comply with all council's plans, rules and regulations? If not, find out what the discrepancies are and why they were allowed.
- Were council officers unhappy with any aspect of the development application or the consent?

Defensive strategies

In gathering your evidence for preparation of an objection, consider these actions:

- Speak to other **affected neighbours**. Enlist their support for your objection if they are not prepared to lodge written objections of their own. (Ask them to co-sign your letter.)
- Lobby local **councillors** to crush the development or to impose conditions on any consent. Take along a **petition** if you can get the signatures.
- Find out if council has a procedure for **mediation** and consider initiating a conference.
- Ask to **address council** or its delegated decision-maker (a committee or officer) before a decision is made.
- Take your concerns to the **local press**.
- If the decision does not go your way, ask council officers about the process for **appeal or review**.
- Prepare a **written objection** and lodge it, on time, with council.

Your objection has a number of aims. First and foremost, you want to get into the loop and maintain your position. Even if you are comfortable with the proposal, you should be aware that a DA frequently changes in potentially material ways as it moves through the investigation process and through the construction period. Windows and doors shift locations, building materials alter, roof elevations and materials differ, and so on. You have to check the proposal at every stage.

Second, you want to let your neighbour know that you are not going to lie down and let them run over the top of you. By making a formal submission, you are declaring that you are vigilant, ready, willing and able to defend your turf—they must take you seriously.

Third, you must choose whether to attack the development *in total* or to press for constructive changes; alternatively, of course, you could support the proposal. There's nothing wrong with going on the record as a supporter—provided you make clear you are supporting the *current form* of the development application. State that you are reserving your right to object to any alteration or amendment.

In my experience, it is difficult to get an entire development application hit on the head if it is residential. However, great success can be found in making a case for 'fair' changes to the plans and in placing conditions on the consent. Further, it is quite possible to appear to support your neighbour's application while at the same time calling for changes and conditions which are either so fundamental to the design or so costly to implement that, if approved in this form, the neighbour could not proceed with the development.

The written objection

Before you start writing, see whether council has a factsheet or other information on how to prepare a submission. You should do the following:

- Check the **zoning** and compare the **permitted use** of the site with the proposed use. For example, is the owner wanting to change the use of the property—perhaps from residential to commercial or, if already commercial, from a fruit shop to a takeaway food outlet or office? The zoning conditions will tell you whether this use or change of use is permitted without council approval or whether approval must be sought.
- Run through the various **development controls** and check the mathematics of them. These will include: setbacks from boundaries; the floorspace ratio; building height; number of car parking spaces; areas of landscaping; positioning of things like air-conditioning units, and so on.

- Deal with those factors which are **discretionary** or which relate to issues of the **merit** of the proposal: overshadowing, bulk, access to light, amenity of the area, suitability of the design (how it relates to the streetscape and general area), how it affects views, noise issues, odour issues, public health, privacy (location of doors, windows, decks and entertainment areas).

These matters will form the basis of your objection.

✓ *Tip:* Style tips for your objection:

- Keep it short and to the point.
- Refer to planning rules, preferably **by number**. Compare measurements **by numbers**. Don't wander too far without anchoring your submission in specifics.
- Refer to the plans and **supporting documentation**.
- Concentrate on the **crunch points**, not on tiny discrepancies.
- Be **unemotional** in tone—this is not the place or time for a slanging match.
- Be helpful—suggest a way forward or a **compromise** which could be acceptable to all.

Getting consent

When the DA comes to council or to a committee or delegated officer for consideration, it will be accompanied by one or more reports from council officers. These will cover the technical aspects of the proposal (compliance with local plans, zoning, drainage issues, etc.) and will deal briefly with submissions received from neighbours and the public. It is likely there will be a recommendation from council officers to approve or reject the application.

Councillors do not always follow the advice of the officers. This is where behind-the-scenes lobbying pays off. Councillors are prepared to take a political view. Somewhere during the process, the developer might amend and resubmit modified plans in order to improve the chances of success. Keep an eye out for this—you don't want to be in the position of arguing the case for an objection which no longer has validity.

There are conditions attached by council to all development consents. They will cover matters such as permitted hours when construction can take place, noise, landscaping, setbacks to boundaries, height restrictions, overshadowing of neighbouring properties, vehicle accommodation, floorspace ratios, waste removal, kerbing and guttering, insurance and much more. And there will be fees (see Chapter 10 for an illustration).

If the developer is unhappy with the result from council—either the DA is declined or the conditions are unacceptable—there is an avenue of appeal. Council or your solicitor will notify you of this and of the time limit for lodging an appeal.

Hired gun: The town planning consultant

What is a town planning consultant? Do you need one? The short answer is: if you don't know the answers to these two questions, then yes, you probably do need one on your side.

Town planning consultants lead an almost invisible life to the property investment community. You usually find out about them when you've got yourself into trouble. Typically, when planning a property project, we find someone who becomes our touchstone, our guide through the process. Dangerously, this person might be a real estate agent—who has an ongoing personal financial (commission-based) interest in your project—or a 'technician'. By technician I mean a person whose view of the process is rooted in a technical task such as surveying, conveyancing or assessing the tax implications.

These are all necessary members of your team of advisers. But there is always the risk that their viewpoints are narrow, merely slices of the overall picture. A good town planning consultant is in a position to give you perhaps the most valuable view of all: a roadmap for getting the development across the consent line. And as soon as that is achieved, you have already made money—you have a more valuable property on your hands.

These people have professional qualifications in town planning. Importantly, most of them have at some stage been employed by local councils or planning organisations. The good ones continue to get contract work from local councils—things like performing strategic studies to review land use and subdivision criteria. They know how the process works from the other side of the counter. If they work in the area of your project, they will also know many of the elected councillors and the senior staff at council—who is easy to get on with, who is going to be a problem and requires special care and attention. They know who you should focus your lobbying effort on.

As noted earlier, there is always a danger that your technical experts can overreach, can try too hard to give you something special. In so doing, they might transgress not just the requirements of local and regional planning instruments, but the 'unwritten' policies which council interprets and applies when making decisions. A well-connected town planner will be aware of all this and should be able to lead you through the minefield.

Strategies for using a town planning consultant

There are three main ways you might use a town planning consultant on your project:

1 **To write the development application for you**. The consultant will endeavour to pre-empt problems by addressing council's expectations right from the start. He or she will ensure you lodge *all* the necessary bits and pieces, your plans and annexures and so on, together with things like your 'statement of environmental effects'. This avoids needless delay and hassle. They will ensure the deadlines are met.

2 **To handle objectors and objections**. Your consultant will become the conduit for all correspondence from council, its officers and any objectors. He or she will prepare appropriate responses—of a technical nature where this helps. Obviously you would discuss the objections with your town planner. They will supply the words and technical terminology to frame your rebuttal. They will become your advocate, arguing the case for your project.

Clearly this has the ancillary benefit of focusing the concerns of neighbours or the wider local community on the town planner rather than on you. You can take at least a small step back from the frontline and give yourself some breathing space with your neighbours.

If necessary, they will call a mediation meeting with objectors and council officers to try to find an acceptable solution which will keep the development moving forward. Would you want to chair such a meeting yourself? As one town planner put it to me recently, people are much more aware these days that they have 'rights', and are more prepared to stand up and get their opinions and objections heard. They might be technically wrong about the limited rights they have to take part in the council planning approvals process, but that is no answer. A particular concern is where council officers respond to objectors by arranging meetings and assisting in one way or another. 'Effectively,' said this town planner, 'council is inviting objectors into the approvals process, even in some states or on occasions where there is no legal right to do so. The objectors feel empowered and can take over the process if council officers—and the developer applicant—are not alert and in control.'

3 **Be your expert witness**. If the development hits a major snag, but you still want to continue, the town planning consultant will become your expert witness at all forums—from sessions with council officers or councillors, to mediation with objectors or, ultimately, in the appeals court.

Some types of development, particularly in their specific planned location, are doomed to a bumpy ride from the start. For example, there was a development application to run the business of a brothel which ended up in the appeals court unnecessarily. Council officers had advised the councillors that there was no power to deny the application—it complied with all requirements. Yet, for local political reasons, council rejected the development. In so doing, it passed the buck to the appeals court, which would now be the body to deliver the approval. Council had washed its hands of ultimate responsibility.

You don't have to be planning a brothel to find yourself in the same situation. A matter as simple as a new front fence—if it is not 'sympathetic' to the heritage style prevalent in the street—can find its way to an appeals court for the final go-ahead. In any potentially controversial development project, it is wise to get your town planning consultant on board from the start.

A less compromised perspective

Nadia purchased a large home and yard with a view to future development as a townhouse site.

'This will be my superannuation,' she said. 'When the land has appreciated sufficiently I will either sell it to a developer or, more likely, do the development myself. The estate agent who handled the purchase has shown me a similarly sized block which now boasts a charming four-townhouse development.

'Two-storey buildings maximise the value we can shoehorn on to the site and provide the opportunity for more heritage-type features such as iron lacework and french doors. The agent believes townhouses like these will really stand out in the local market, which is pretty basic in design really, and will sell well.'

Her bank was keen to lend her the million or so dollars she would require to complete the development. 'But a quick sale will be very important to me. I can't carry a million-dollar-plus mortgage for long on my salary!'

Because Nadia didn't have the time to handle many of the aspects of the development herself, she engaged a town planning consultant. One of the first things the consultant told her was the sorry history of two-storey homes in that suburb. It was an area where vacant land was still relatively cheap. This meant that property owners got more bang for their buck by spreading out horizontally. Building vertically cost more and was more expensive to maintain over time. Many investors shunned two-storey properties because they cut out (in their opinion) a large and growing segment of both tenants and potential owners: retirees and the aged. Ground-level homes had a broader appeal, it was said.

The town planner ran through a number of local examples where developers had found difficulty selling their two-storey townhouses. In some cases, the developer had tried two or three times without success to auction what were essentially brand-new two-storey homes. This led to price cuts, delays and strife at the bank.

It was not the angle which Nadia had been hearing from her real estate agent. Perhaps the potential sales commission had clouded the issue.

A town planning consultant will work for you at an hourly rate or for a set fee negotiated in advance. An hourly rate can be brought in to sort out matters which expand from their initial limits. As a rough guide, you can expect to pay of the order of $1000 to $3000 (depending on location, the consultant's overheads, etc.) for assistance with preparing and lodging the development application, and much the same for negotiating the objections. It isn't a huge amount of money but it's an expense which is easily left out of an investor's calculations.

Dealing with council officers

What have you heard about council officers, the people whose job it is to check a development application against the rules, laws and codes? Lazy bureaucrats? Dumb time-servers? Corrupt administrators? Hard-working professionals? My experience is that you can meet all of the above as you work to get your development approved and constructed. It would certainly be a wrong move to under-estimate their strength of purpose.

On the whole, I have found council officers to be hard-working professionals. I do not envy their workload and the level of stress that falls on those in senior positions, such as the principal town planner. The volume of work they handle can be intense—as are the emotions of the various developers caught up in the process. Too often there are insufficient staff to handle applications within the necessary time limits. This is a source of great friction.

Of course, council officers, sitting astride the bureaucracy, are in a position to really hurt the applicant. Delay, expensive conditions placed on an approval, additional paperwork, lost files . . . there is a well-understood range of techniques that can punish or discourage.

More often, however, I have come to see council officers as people who can cut through the crust on a bogged-down or confused development and be the voice of reason: when all those on your team of experts seem muddled or stalled, I turn to the council officers to find the way forward. Their answers to your desperate questions can be brutal, galling or surprising, but they are also often the precise reference points you need.

Architects, designers, builders, engineers, lawyers, town planning consultants and anyone else on your payroll are trying to please you, to keep you keen on progressing the development. And when the project hits a wall with council, *your* people may not always tell you the things they believe you don't want to hear. In many cases, in my experience, your own experts are not clear on the planning law requirements in the first place—and that's why your project gets bogged down.

Designing your way into trouble

You go to your site with your architect, or the agent trying to sell you the property, and take a good look around. You see what the neighbours have done with their properties—boundary setbacks, size of buildings, placement of garages, landscaping, driveway access, etc.—and plan to take advantage of their precedent value to do similar things with your development. 'If council has already approved something nearby, well they can't object to us doing the same thing!'

On the contrary. One local government councillor from a major Sydney suburb who was interviewed for this book had this to say by way of warning:

> Look at what is possible *now*, not what was done three, five, ten years ago. You can't rely on precedent. Planning controls may well have changed and you must comply with the current rules. For example, your property might now have a heritage listing or be in a conservation area; development standards might have changed.

Planning and construction requirements are not static. Even if the black-and-white words on council planning documents have remained unchanged for some years you will find there is a whole parallel universe of 'background chatter' and policy-making which will influence not just future standards but the interpretation of the current rules. There is a substantial degree of flexibility in the wording of planning instruments and guides which allows council and its officers to steer development on to a desired course. The smart developer understands that it is vital to find out from council officers what the 'new thinking' for your area is—what principles and unwritten policies are influencing the decision-making.

For example, according to this councillor: 'Energy efficiency is becoming a very, very big design issue for councils. Many architects we see do not understand this.' The councillor pointed to a trend towards the use of very large windows to take advantage of views. There are significant privacy and energy issues resulting from this trend and councils pore over DA plans which go this way. 'Consideration for neighbours has become a major policy concern for council. This means extra expense for the developer or a curtailing of the extent of the approval council will grant,' he said. A common flashpoint with Sydney councils is the placement of air-conditioning compressors near a neighbour's bedroom. Council will either reject the move or require acoustic baffles of some kind—along with a certificate from an acoustics engineer that the design work reduces the noise of the compressor to the required level.

As well as council's requirements, investors should realise the impact of the Building Code of Australia. This important document, which sets many of the building and construction standards adopted by councils, is updated regularly. Environmental controls are becoming increasingly technical so that property designs must achieve a number of aims: to reduce the electricity and gas we use; to increase the use of solar power; to increase the use of water-saving appliances and attachments; to increase the use of insulating materials; to reduce the transfer of heat and cold through walls, and so on. Council will knock you back if your plans do not comply with the Building Code of Australia, so discuss this document with your architect or designer.

Council concern for your neighbours also now extends, in many areas, to the preservation of views. In the past, the general rule was that no one had a *right* to a view. The understanding was that if all existing views were maintained by law then development would be stifled. Now the position is quite different. Not only are councils placing conditions on approvals designed to preserve a property owner's views (even if just in part); they are concerned about loss of views to the public on the street. This presents a design issue which, again, can be hard to discern from the bald planning documents.

The issue is one of 'loss of a significant public view'. Here's an example. For 50 years, residents strolling down your street to the corner shop have wandered past detached houses which alternately obscured then revealed the dense bushland or water view beyond. The pleasant view flickered past. Along comes a developer who wants to pull down seven of the houses and erect a most pleasing, and currently fashionable, row of terrace 'mansions' in the Georgian style. However, strollers will no longer enjoy the flickering vista—there will just be a massive slab of concrete rendering. And that is a loss of a significant public view. Council will have words to say to you about this.

A further area of concern to councillors is that first-time 'developers' can find they have purchased the wrong property. 'It is common for me to find myself standing out on the street at an inspection,' says my councillor, 'when the would-be developer turns to me and says: "Well, my solicitor didn't tell me about this when we purchased the property!"'

Properties can have an extensive range of encumbrances on the legal title. There may be an **easement** for the sewer pipes or storm water, a **right of way** for a neighbour to drive or walk upon, or a **covenant** specifying what building materials or fencing can or cannot be used (see Chapter 6). Your conveyancer should spot these matters on the legal title to the property you are buying, but their importance can sometimes be lost—particularly if you have not made clear to your conveyancer that you are intending to develop or redesign the site at some point in time. These encumbrances sound old-fashioned and it is tempting to switch off when your conveyancer mentions them. But they are still in use today—and they will affect **what** you can build, **where** you can build on the site and **what materials** you might have to use.

The list of encumbrances is expanding in the light of more recent catastrophes. For example, an area of low-lying land, full of houses and flats, might now be classified as a 'flood plain'. Despite all the existing homes, future development might either be prohibited or subject to expensive construction conditions and limitations. Similarly, the spate of devastating bushfires in areas like the Blue Mountains west of Sydney or Canberra has resulted in a re-evaluation of building standards. A bushfire-prone zone will have rules about the style of construction, choice of building materials, setbacks from bushland and more. There are also areas emerging which are burdened with a kind of black listing by insurance companies—you can buy the home, but you can't insure it (or the premium is extravagant).

Natural disasters are resulting in the creation of what might be called **environmental encumbrances**. Clearly these have the potential to savage your planning budget or to turn a once-valuable development site into an economically void plot.

The second trap with conveyancing is to believe that your solicitor or conveyancer is investigating everything that might affect your property. The reality is that the conveyancing process is focused on a single property. Your neighbour could be boiling up meat carcasses and offal to manufacture salami (don't laugh—this is a true example) and you won't find out about it from your solicitor or conveyancer.

Similarly, you won't necessarily be told that a neighbour has lodged a DA with council to put on a second storey or add a pool, radically affecting your quiet, sunny spot. Don't rely on anyone to tell you the full story, no matter what you are paying them. You must do the detective work yourself, going to council and prowling the area by day and night. When the wind changes direction, for example, you could find that the flightpath shifts over the top of your property. Is there a plan for a new road or highway nearby? Council town planning and building officers are the first people you should see.

There are a number of key reasons to get on side with council's officers. You will uncover information about:

- the history of the site;
- potential heritage or environmental issues;

- whether other development proposals for the site have succeeded or failed and why;
- whether there are any council objectives or desires for the site and its general area—in other words, council priorities;
- compromises which council might accept;
- what the neighbours are doing—what else has been approved or is under discussion for development nearby;
- contacts for local lobby groups;
- whether the written development control plans, zoning plans and developer guidelines are still the best reference for your work. Typically there are new planning laws, control plans or amendments at some stage of development;
- how to fast-track your application.

The approvals process need not be difficult or a mystery. But, amidst all the things you will find out from council officers, there is still room for a fundamental slip. I'll close this chapter with two pieces of advice from experienced active investors.

✓ *Tip:* Make sure you are talking to the **decision-makers** at council. You must work your way back to those whose opinions count.

✓ *Tip:* If a piece of information is vital to your project, **get it in writing** or it is valueless and unreliable.

Of course, this won't always be possible or straightforward—though you might surprise yourself at what can be achieved. You may be able to get a letter from a council officer or be directed to a ruling, court decision, local precedent or section of legislation. Failing this, the next best step is a whole lot better than nothing: take detailed notes of your meetings with council officers. Make them *contemporaneous* (that is, written at the meeting itself, not afterwards from recollection), note the names of all present, and date the notes. I wouldn't go to court on their strength alone but they could just give you a little lift in sticky negotiations down the track.

Summary

- Learn the language of development so you can communicate clearly with council officers and your experts.
- Understand the lodgment process and the objections process.
- Consider engaging a town planning consultant to steer you through the process or to handle any objections.
- Get council officers on side.
- If something is vital, try to get it in writing from council or council's documents.
- Know your rights of appeal against a decision of council.

8

Working with your designer

The design for your construction project is one place where real profit is lurking. Nail the right design and purchasers or tenants will beat a path to your door. In my experience, we start the process of property redesign with every intention of creating a wonderful, beautiful design for the site. It will be stylish, a credit to the neighbourhood and a monument to our good taste. Yet, after the lengthy process of development has run its course, the end result might be something we hope is never traced to our name.

Money, time, stress, objections, faulty building work, our own inexperience—all these and more play a role in this disillusionment. Even when we are fortunate to have created something which is good, we can easily be left with a nagging feeling that some things could have been handled better. Still, you can't expect perfection and you'd go mad if you demanded it from others or from yourself.

There is much we can do to 'get the design right'. In the most pleasing cases, it will be your architect or designer who sets you on this path. We like it when they take our ideas and sketches and bring them to life in technicolour. In entrusting our project—and our financial security—to these experts, we are relying on their knowledge of the rules and their eye for the full potential of the site (within the budget, of course).

It is an imperfect process. In this chapter we will look at:

- the decision whether to use an architect or a designer to draw your plans;
- what it will cost you;
- where things go wrong; and
- how to prepare the 'design brief'.

What does an architect do for you?

The Royal Australian Institute of Architects notes there are typically five stages to an architect's involvement in a project. The first of these is 'initiation':

> The Architect establishes the client's needs, expectations, project requirements and budget. This information is collated to prepare a written document called the design brief.

This should include time and effort to find out from council what can and cannot be done on the site.

The second is the design phase:

> The Architect analyses the design brief and the site conditions, features and constraints and determines the best location and orientation. The Architect begins to develop ideas through rough plans, sketches and models. These ideas are brought together into concept design drawings.

Next comes design development, documentation and gaining a building approval:

> The Architect compares the concept design drawings with the design brief and develops the technical detail for the project with the project team. Detailed drawings and specifications are prepared to enable the builder to construct the project. The drawings are lodged to obtain local authority building approval. The method of engaging a builder for the project is determined.

The fourth stage is one of implementation—the phase where the construction takes place. Here the architect works to ensure the drawings and specifications are followed by the builder. Finally, the architect has an ongoing responsibility, once the building is complete, to chase up any work which should be done by the builder as part of the defects warranty period or otherwise.

A designer or draftsperson can do these tasks but is likely to limit him or herself, particularly during the fourth and fifth stages. Indeed, it might be left to the builder or yourself to lodge the plans with council. You might be able to pay extra to have your designer or draftsperson handle some or all of these steps or you could find they are unwilling and/or uninsured to do this. This news can come as an unwelcome surprise late in the day if you find you need more hands-on assistance with the project, particularly during the construction phase.

Should I use an architect or a designer?

You will need a qualified person—an architect or designer—to prepare your development plans for lodgment with council. The issues involved in choosing between an architect and a designer are set out in Table 8.1.

What it will cost

A draftsperson or drafting service might simply charge a flat fee for the job, or there may be a minimum fee for a small job rather than a straight percentage. Architects generally charge a percentage of the project's value—from 8 per cent to as much as 15 per cent (the smaller the job, the larger the percentage). A design service will charge around a third of this.

The architect's fee would normally cover ongoing supervision of the building work (although you should confirm this when making your arrangements). This could span a time period of twelve to 24 months, so it could turn out to be good value for money to have the architect as intermediary between you and the builders and tradespeople. Discuss with the architect how often he or she will visit the site during construction. Get a clear sense of what services you are getting for your money.

Table 8.1 Architect or designer?

Why choose an architect?	Why choose a designer?
Has professional indemnity insurance which should allow him/her to look after your project from design to completion of construction (if you wish)	A less expensive option (but check that he or she carries indemnity insurance for the tasks you require to be performed)
You are looking for greater experience with original or unusual design elements and materials	Where the job is basic
The value of the project justifies the expense of engaging an architect	If the project is a renovation or extension to match an existing building, many of the design solutions need only be copied
More likely to be familiar with arranging tender processes for the various construction jobs	You want to have a more active role in selecting builders and tradespeople
To detect any problems and ensure they get fixed by the builder; to be your negotiator	You are prepared to work things out with the builder and tradespeople
To be your expert witness in court or before a tribunal if the project is held up by council or if you are in dispute with your builder: a higher level of qualifications is an asset in these circumstances	
To negotiate with council and its officers on approvals and conditions of approval	

It is common for medium-sized or large residential building companies to have a designer on staff. Their fees are absorbed into the cost of the total job of design and construction and are likely to include getting the plans through council. They often promote themselves with the offer of a free 'concept plan'.

Always ascertain whether they will charge for work which does not proceed.

Where things can go wrong

If you've never worked with or commissioned an architect or draftsperson, then you should probably know something about the sorts of problems consumers report. This knowledge will help you when interviewing various candidates for your job. It can seem negative to focus on the problems rather than the solutions these experts offer, but this is not my intention. I have had mostly positive experiences. However, at the end of the day, I can afford to be surprised by a clever design solution but not by a design disaster.

'He doesn't listen to me'

This is one of the most common complaints I've heard. Communication is a problem for most professionals, but it has a certain extra element of frustration when owners are trying to put into words their own artistic vision and concept. Put yourself in the shoes of the architect or designer: they have to take the owner's vague ideas and turn them into something technically workable and within budget. Is it any wonder that at some point they drift off into their own world and appear to have stopped listening?

'She listens too much to me'

Are you the one who is driving the design side of the project? Are you being too forceful? If so, you might just get precisely what you want and not what you need.

'He is stuck in his ways'

Designers have found what works for them—tried and tested solutions to common design problems: flooring, verandahs sheltering the front door, how to bring light into a dark room, a 'signature' roofline, and so on. It can take effort to move them into new territory.

'She is not familiar with new materials and finishes'

Your architect seems to know nothing about the new materials and designs you've found after trawling through a pile of magazines. See if he or she is willing to pick up the phone and do the follow-up.

'His design got me into trouble'

When I was a solicitor, I spent a lot of time going to court over development issues. Early on in a project, when it seemed likely

'It's just what I asked for! I'm so unhappy!'

Aldo and Francesca had bought a dump—and they knew it. But it was in a great location near the coast and had a wonderful garden. The fibro house would be developed straight away, as soon as they moved in, so it really wouldn't be too bad.

They only had enough spare cash (and what they could borrow) to do half the house, but they would do it properly. Sometime later they would finish the job.

Both worked hard, so the priority would be a new loungeroom, dining room and kitchen—an open-plan complex of Cecil B. de Mille proportions. Rapidly they got on with it. It was a furious time of researching shower screens, doorway mechanisms, light fittings, chic benchtop materials and the rest. Meanwhile they lived in the daggy back section of their home.

The home was in a part of Australia which was very windy, with harsh winters and summers—very cold, then very hot. But they wanted lots of glass—after all, they had purchased the place in large part because of the beautiful garden. 'We wanted to see it all the time, from wherever we were,' said Francesca. 'And we wanted a lifestyle where the line between the indoors and outdoors was blurred.'

The architect delivered what they wanted. *Precisely* what they had asked for. (They had been very particular, and their brief was comprehensive.)

A year after completion of that crucial first half of the redevelopment, a somewhat cruel acquaintance pointed out that they had built their loungeroom/dining room/kitchen complex on the wrong side of the house: towards the south-west.

'We realised this was true,' said Francesca. 'Although there were acres of glass, we got no winter sun. The room was dark and cold. Then, in the summer, all we got was afternoon sun. The room was hot and stuffy.

'Our energy costs were enormous, with a high level of heating in the winter and air-conditioning in the summer.'

Their home is still lovely, with beautiful fittings and loads of clever design features. 'But why didn't the architect get us to place the living areas on the right side of the house?' asked Francesca. 'He must have known, given our climate, that there would be problems.'

that court action was inevitable, I would grill the architect about the plans. 'Do the plans conform to *all* of council's development standards and regulations?' I would ask. Invariably the architect replied: 'Of course'. Yet in the courtroom, with council's town planner in the witness box, it would come out that the plans breached one or more of the planning regulations. The wrong floorspace ratio, overshadowing of another's property, side set-backs—many of these points were matters of simple mathematics. And the architect's response? 'Well, the plans might be *technically* in breach of the regulations, but they are totally within the *spirit* of the regulations.'

'He won't let me tender the job with other tradespeople'

Watch out for this little trap: whoever creates the plans will generally own the copyright in them. If you use a design service run by a builder, you must make it clear from the start if you want to seek quotes from other builders or use tradespeople of your own choice. The building company might claim ownership of the plans and maintain control over who does what. This is fine if you want them to do everything for you; however, if this is not your intention, discuss your needs and put any understandings in writing before the design work commences.

Mistakes with measurements

Council was not happy. It had looked at the figures supplied by Terri and her husband for their renovation and had come up with different numbers. Council saw it as a typical case of a try-on from greedy home owners who wanted too much from a site! It was going to squash them for their deceptive ways.

Terri didn't understand what was going wrong. After all, they had left everything in the hands of their architect. They looked at the plans and all the measurements seemed fine. Now council was saying they had understated the amount of the site they wanted to develop.

The architect took to council's officers with a vengeance. He argued that his plans were perfect—and that the officers should work harder on their maths. It soon bubbled through to Terri that this approach was not winning friends or influencing people.

In a conciliatory move, and to get the project back on track, she had a private meeting with the council officers. Here they pointed out to her what her architect had failed to tell her: the architect's scale was incorrect. While the plan said the drawings were to a nominated scale, in reality this was not true. The plans showed a development which, on all figures, went 10 per cent in excess of the allowances. This was not immediately apparent—the discrepancy only appeared when going through the calculations in detail.

As it turned out, the architect had misprogrammed part of his software. It said one thing but did another. Even the architect didn't know he was making this mistake. He would have to reprogram his computerised equipment and prepare a fresh set of plans.

✓ *Tip:* Be specific about what you want but be open-minded about how the architect/designer delivers this.

The design brief

The design brief is the document you use to commission your architect, draftsperson or designer. When there's a mess-up later on, this is the place you will look to see if someone has done the wrong thing. Clearly, the more specific and comprehensive you are, the better your chances of having someone else clean up the problem.

There is no set form for the brief, but these are some headings which I find helpful.

Preliminaries

This opening section is not the place to provide the specifics—it's where you establish your general principles. For example, 'to be energy efficient', 'to blend into the natural environment', 'to be true to the architectural style of the rest of the building', 'to provide the utmost privacy and security', 'a lovely, warm and inviting family home', 'a cool, hip, contemporary home using innovative design solutions'.

The building

Here you will set out the basic numbers and features of your development. For example, that there will be four bedrooms, two bathrooms (one ensuite to main bedroom), large kitchen, open-plan lounge and dining opening to the view of the valley. Or 'three townhouses each with two bedrooms, ensuite . . .'

Will the main bathroom have a tub or spa? Will the ensuite have a shower but no bath? Will the bedrooms all be large? Do you want a deck off the back door? Give the ceiling height, the corridor widths and all key measurements which define your requirements. You will probably prepare this section in consultation with your architect/designer.

Grounds and landscaping

Be specific about plants, garden beds, protection from wind and exposure to sun, water features, paving, watering systems, drainage and so on.

Building materials

This is the place to describe the *look* you are after. Is the property or development to follow a well-understood historic style of architecture such as Federation, Victorian terrace, Frank Lloyd Wright? Contemporary? Tuscan? Oz beach shack?

Separate the interior from the exterior. List the materials that are important to you—for example, stone, brick, cement sheets, plaster board, slate, carpet, cork tiles, timber flooring, aluminium or timber windows and doors, fly screens, lighting (halogen, downlights, fluorescent tubes, period light fittings).

This section could proceed room by room, area by area. Be specific.

- Name the brands and model numbers for appliances—for example, 'Miele Novotronic W 828'.
- Specify where things are to go: power points, taps, light fittings, switches, intercom or security equipment, TV antenna access, phone and internet access points, and so on.
- With floor coverings, specify which way the carpet pile or overlaps will run, which way tile patterns are to be laid, etc.

- If relevant, specify which way the doors are to open and from which jamb they are hinged.
- Include sketches and photographs—from magazines, product brochures or taken in friends' homes—to explain not simply what you want, but how the finished job is to look.
- In an addition or extension, are the new windows, architraves, skirting, cornices, and so on to match existing ones precisely? Need they be the same brands and models?
- Are built-in robes to have backs and sides? Or is it enough to use the exposed wall surfaces?

Vehicle accommodation

How many car spaces? Will they be open, under cover or secure? How will vehicles move around the property? Will there be a turning circle? You might not know where you want the garage to go, but if you want to avoid nasty surprises you might consider saying where you do *not* want it to go.

Getting things round the right way

The client had purchased a building block with a superb water view. The block fell away towards the view and down from the road above. The draftsman was briefed to design a modest three-bedroom home with garaging for two cars.

The first full plans for the house were a revelation. The house plan was entirely typical of thousands of others: along one side ran the important rooms (master bedroom, loungeroom, kitchen) and along the other side were the less glamorous rooms (laundry, pantry, garage, the smallest bedroom).

However, the loungeroom, master bedroom and kitchen faced the 'front' of the house—the roadway. And the view (which was in the opposite direction) was obscured by the large two-car garage. If you wanted to enjoy the magnificent water views from inside the house you had to go into the laundry, where there was a small window positioned high on the wall.

The draftsman had simply taken his normal three-bedroom home plan and whacked it on the block so the front door faced the road entrance. Single-handedly he had inadvertently set out on a course to halve the value of the property.

Environmental issues

Do you want the property to conform to an energy rating scheme (e.g. 'five star rating')? Consideration should also be made of issues such as the use of grey water, solar heating and hot water, low-flow toilets and shower heads, heating and cooling appliances and methods, double glazing or use of special glass products, collection of rainwater from the roof, recycling facility, noise reduction technologies, insulation materials and so on.

Level of finish

This is the section where you should indicate whether you just want something which will sell quickly, if the finishes must be sufficiently robust to endure years of tenancy, or whether you are working to a strict budget and will accept a basic job. State your budget. If you're after a Rolls Royce finish, you should make this clear or all sorts of compromises will automatically find their way into the plans and specifications.

Check the details

Brad's renovation was pretty straightforward, so he decided he didn't need an architect—just a local draftsman. Brad instructed the draftsman to give the main bedroom a large walk-in robe. By this, Brad meant he wanted more clothes hanging space overall. What he also meant—but didn't say—was that he was fed up with carefully ironing his clothes only to find they got crushed in the tight space of his current walk-in robe.

The draftsman duly put a larger robe in the plans. It was only when Brad, on a whim, got out his ruler that he found the hanging space depth—from shoulder to shoulder across a jacket, for example—was narrower than he wanted. It was only 50 centimetres. The current robe (which was unacceptable) provided 55 centimetres and Brad realised he probably wanted 65 centimetres.

Brad felt relieved to have discovered the problem before work began. He thought that in telling the draftsman he wanted a large walk-in robe he would get a generously proportioned hanging space. Instead, the draftsman fell back on the usual dimensions he used with his regular clients and simply gave Brad more length but not more depth.

What you require of the designer

Set out the tasks you want your designer to perform for you. These might include all or just some of the tasks referred to earlier in the chapter.

Attachments

If you've done some sketches, include them here. Simply attach them so they form part of the brief—they become part of your instructions. Your architect or designer should take the opportunity to discuss your drawings if there is a problem before he or she gets too far along with the plans.

Finally, keep a copy of the brief for your own use and reference.

Cross-cultural problem-solving

Three architects later, Don and Yukio believe they finally have the design they wanted for their home and studio extension.

'When we were looking for a home, maybe eight years ago, we thought property prices were high in Sydney. Things haven't changed!' said Don. 'We found the suburb we wanted to live in—near the upper reaches of Sydney Harbour—but we had to decide whether to stretch ourselves financially and buy on the waterfront or whether to act more responsibly and buy a few blocks back.

'The waterfront home would have cost us a small fortune—a bit over $400 000. In the end we opted for a small cottage around half a kilometre from the water, in the mid-$200 000 range.

'Now, after a substantial extension we put on five years ago—a huge family lounge, wrap-around verandahs, open fireplace—our home is worth, say, $800 000. And the waterfront home we passed on? It's $1.2–1.5 million dollars. We've done well, but you can't help thinking . . .'

At the time Don and his Japanese-born wife Yukio purchased their home, Don was self-employed and Yukio was working in someone else's business. Their small home suited them fine. Once children came along, they needed more space and put on the extension.

'Now I am the employee and my wife has her own business. She became interested in quilting and runs courses for students two nights per week. Her business has become very successful. This means more students and huge storage issues for materials and pieces in the process of cutting and sewing. If we had anticipated this use for the property we might well have purchased quite a different property,' said Don. 'Now it is our only major asset and we have had to reshape it to work better both as a home and a workplace with substantial numbers of visitors.

'It is a mix of residential and commercial uses. To fit them all in, we needed to go up.

'The first architect was very helpful. Soon it became apparent he was not merely helpful, he was sycophantic. Whatever we suggested—no matter how way out—he would agree to. He kept saying: "Yes, we can do that".

'He was so intent on satisfying Yukio's wishes that the plans descended into chaos. Clearly he didn't want to upset the customer *over anything*. He was so *positive*. But, with hindsight, he could have led us down some unhelpful and expensive pathways. So we tried another architect.

'The second architect was a person who was prepared to say "no". This was a kind of relief. He would refer to "principles" and "functionality" in answer to our suggestions. We felt we were making progress at last.

'For example, when he first walked into our house he sized up—and communicated to us—the issues. In the hallway he saw "wasted space"; in the kitchen, "wasted space". Our beautiful new living-room extension? "Built on the wrong side of the house—facing the westerly sun." It was shattering.

'He explained things like why the staircase should be in a certain position; where the landing should go. And he openly admitted it when he didn't have an answer. What he taught us was the importance of having an architect with local knowledge, particularly of council policies—written and unwritten.

'Because our home was near the harbour, he warned us there might be special drainage requirements imposed by council. In our own discussions with council officers no one had mentioned this possibility to us. So we commissioned him to do some new plans for the second storey and alterations to the ground floor.

'Sure enough, council told us to get a drainage diagram for the site. We engaged a civil engineer with hydraulics experience. This cost us an unexpected $2500. Our complaint, if you like, was that although our architect had warned us of the possible requirement for special drainage plans and works, he did not alert us to the likely cost.

'But, ultimately, Yukio wasn't happy with his designs. Something was wrong with the façade—the look of the front of the house—with its new second storey. She didn't know what the problem was, and that made it difficult to discuss or to work on. It just wasn't pleasing to her eye. A mass of angles and dormer windows. He gave us a proportional design—everything fitted. But the front was stark and geometric.

'Just as things got bogged down, with no solution in sight, a friend suggested we engage a Japanese-trained architect. As strange as it might seem, there was a real difference. We found that he didn't start out with a classic Australian framework for cottage design. We weren't bouncing around between "Californian bungalow", "Federation" and other local conventions and styles. We believe that he had a better eye for proportion because he was not culturally bound by what was common in Sydney architecture. For example, he suggested a quite different roofline which worked well to fit things in below.

'He suggested small adjustments to the use of spaces—he was quite prepared to let things be smaller in order to deliver a benefit elsewhere. For example, he made a hallway slightly narrower—on a Japanese home scale—and rotated an entrance to provide more functional space.

'And he made the façade more friendly, more ornate and inviting. It was just what we wanted to see,' said Don. 'In the end, he simply gave us a different visual perspective and more options. We broke out of the mould by crossing cultures.'

I've seen the plans for Don and Yukio's house and can understand what Don is talking about. There were some very tricky design issues involved in this project, in part because the property had an increasing home business use at the heart of what was really just a modest suburban cottage. Attempts by local architects to 'fit everything in' had resulted in fairly stilted, lumpy designs. Don and Yukio did not want the stereotypical Sydney second-storey addition, but this is what they were being served. They felt trapped by the language and design elements of local architecture.

Summary

- It's your choice: architect, design service or draftsperson? Private or associated with a building company? There are significant differences in qualifications, price and the services they offer.

- Be clear about whether you want your architect or designer to negotiate with council or supervise the construction phase. Sort out the fee in advance.
- Learn from the experience of friends in dealing with designers and architects. It is very instructive and great preparation.
- Take your time. Think through all the possibilities before you act on anything suggested by your designer or architect. Limit your surprises.
- Be very specific about what you want, but be open-minded about how the architect delivers this.
- Put serious effort into preparation of the design brief. It will rescue you later.
- If you want something unusual but can't get anything other than meat-and-three-veg designs, consider briefing an architect with overseas experience or one who has a different set of cultural reference points.

9

Working with the builder

People like to buy new things—cars, washing machines, computers—because they believe they are getting them in perfect condition. Of course, that's a dubious proposition and never more so than in the case of building work. Unless there has been a deliberate cover-up, older buildings wear their faults on their faces. You might have to engage an expert inspector to find the problems, but this is no drama. New building work, by contrast, can take a little time to reveal what has gone wrong.

Should you be worried as an investor about to enter into a construction contract? Absolutely. The builder is the wild card in your deck. This is a part of the project you can't control. You can lead, you can entice and encourage, you can negotiate—but you can't control.

In 2002, the Archicentre released results of its study of 200 new homes under five years old. It had inspected the newish homes to determine the rates of various faults. What it found—and told the rest of us outside the industry—is remarkable:

- 19 per cent of the homes had roofing problems;
- 11 per cent had damp;
- 10 per cent showed cracking;
- 5 per cent had framing problems.

If this happened to your brand new home, you would be annoyed when you discovered the problem. You would look to your contractual rights against the builder and get on the phone. But as an investor you might not be the one to find the fault first. It will be the person who buys from you, or their tenant, or your tenant if you keep the property. First they will come looking to you—not the builder—to fix the problem. Second, they might not tell you when they notice that something is wrong; the damage could get worse.

As investors, we can reasonably assume we have a one-in-five chance of having a serious building defect show up within the first five years of existence of each separate dwelling we have created. Note also from the survey that these problems seem to have slipped past the initial defects rectifying period at the end of the construction phase (generally lasting from three to six months after practical completion of the work).

Accordingly, we must start the process with as many rights and protections as we can muster, including these:

- Deal only with **licensed** builders and tradespeople.
- Get written and signed **contracts** with everyone.
- Check their work for you is **insured**.
- Check that both the **builders** and **tradespeople** carry their own **insurance**.

Don't be embarrassed about checking these details. While the contracts should cover this situation in detail, the best way to avoid trouble later is to *see* the insurance policies, *see* the dates on receipts for payment of premium, *see* the building or trade licences.

Making a contract

There are several alternative building contracts out there. Most are prepared by industry groups—for builders, architects, tradespeople. In my experience these documents betray a tendency to look after their own people first. Inquire at your consumer affairs or fair trading agency about contracts which do not carry an industry pedigree. It is wise to get expert legal advice on the contract before you sign it. Don't short-change yourself at this point. This is your

Who regulates or licenses builders?

To find out whether your builder is licensed or registered, go to these agencies:

- **Australian Capital Territory**: ACT Planning and Licensing Authority (ACTPLA), builders' licensing section, phone (02) 6207 6273, www.actpla.act.gov.au;
- **New South Wales**: Department of Fair Trading, phone 13 32 20 or (02) 9895 0111, www.fairtrading.nsw.gov.au;
- **Northern Territory**: Department of Infrastructure, Planning and Environment—Building Advisory Services, phone (08) 8999 5511, www.lpe.nt.gov.au. At the time of writing there is no licensing scheme, but it is anticipated that a scheme will be introduced in 2004;
- **Queensland**: the Queensland Building Services Authority (BSA), phone (07) 3225 2800, www.bsa.qld.gov.au;
- **South Australia**: Office of Consumer and Business Affairs, Builders Licensing, phone (08) 8204 9644, www.ocba.sa.gov.au;
- **Tasmania**: Department of Infrastructure, Energy & Resources. It is not a general licensing system, but a scheme for accreditation of the 'principal builder' on the site. Phone (03) 6233 8011, www.wst.tas.gov.au/building;
- **Western Australia**: Builders Registration Board, phone (08) 9476 1200, www.brb.org.au.

opportunity to negotiate amendments for your own increased protection.

When you enter a construction contract, be aware that there are rights and responsibilities on *both* sides. A failure on your part will justify action by the builder to suspend work, to cancel the contract and walk away, to extend the deadline or to charge extra. Note what the builder owes you, what you owe the builder, and where the fights are.

How to handle contractual variations

When a renovation or building moves from two-dimensional paper plans to three-dimensional reality, we all see things from a radical

Table 9.1 Understanding rights and responsibilities

Contractual hot spots	Rights and fights
What the builder owes you	• To work in a proper and workmanlike manner in accordance with the plans and specifications • To use materials which are 'suitable for the purpose' for which they are supplied • To use only new materials (unless otherwise agreed) • To finish the job on time or within a reasonable time • To provide a dwelling that is fit for occupation • To comply with relevant laws • To finish the job on budget as quoted and varied by agreement
What you owe the builder	• Payment on time • Clear instructions • Proper access to the site
Where the fights occur	• Variations—extra or different work • Delay—starting or finishing late • Quality of the work • Getting defects fixed • Interpretation of instructions • Incomplete or late payment

new perspective. Maybe a doorway should be moved 50 centimetres to the left to fit in a built-in wardrobe. Are the power points in the best positions? We're going to need to get more light into the ensuite.

If you've done some serious building or renovation work before, you will know that problems arise almost every day. And they need to be resolved fast or you will lose the tiler, plumber, bricklayer or electrician for two weeks while he moves on to his next job. Of course, if the renovation is for your own home it is easy to get swept along in the excitement and decide to add little improvements here and there as things take shape. This is not just a possibility—it is to be expected. Accordingly, a little extra money needs to be set aside for such 'variations to the contract' right from the start.

If the variation is done in a rush, it effectively leap-frogs an elaborate planning process. It is surprisingly easy to get it wrong.

Here's a true story. The builder and plumber are installing a new hot water service and tub in the laundry. The new models are smaller than the old ones, so suddenly there is some extra space in the room. The owners think: 'We could fit a second toilet in there! There's only one toilet in the whole house at the moment. What a relief that would be!' A quick discussion follows. The plumber says he can do it for 'about an extra thousand'. The owners look at each other for a second and say 'Yes'. Then they head off to work with a picture in their minds.

Coming home that evening, all is quiet. The builder and plumber had left a couple of hours earlier. The owners rush through the front door and into the laundry, then stop in horror. The new toilet faces right into the doorway. 'That's crazy! Why would anyone put it there? It should have gone on the other wall—that's the logical position for it!' Not only was the toilet installed on the wrong wall, at 90 degrees to the desired angle and in full view of the hallway outside, but the builder had squeezed the cistern under a window, necessitating the removal of half the moulded architrave.

As far as the owners were concerned, it could not have been more wrong if they had stuck the toilet on the roof. But there had been no solid, clear discussion about positioning the toilet. That's because the location had seemed *obvious*. Ten weeks later, the bills came. The plumber charged $1150—only $150 above the quoted price (but then, even the owners knew it was off the top of his head). Yet it was out by 15 per cent. And the builder charged an extra $200 for his time ('wrecking the window!') and management of the plumber. All up, it was a 35 per cent overshoot. But the owners had no come-back. The work was done well and the materials were of commercial quality.

When the owner wants something new, extra or different from the approved plans, this is a variation of the contract with the builder. The contract will say how variations are to be made. Generally this includes:

- putting the instruction in writing;
- attaching relevant specifications if necessary;

- a statement of how much time this will extend the contract deadline;
- getting everyone to sign the variation: owner, builder and, where relevant, architect or construction supervisor;
- stating the extra cost or how the work is to be priced;
- noting the date of the variation.

Attach the written variation to the contract. Add a sketch plan if this would help identify with greater precision what and where you want something new to happen. The plan can be very simple—a square for the room with crosses showing the locations of power points. For jobs where the visual impact is important, it is good to sketch a floorplan and a view of how the room should look. Will the fireplace be set flush with the wall or inset into the room? Will the new doorway open into the kitchen or into the pantry? Will the kitchen tap be positioned on the sink or off the wall? Will the floor tiles be laid straight or on the diagonal?

Delays

Planning an addition to your home or a set of townhouses can become an all-consuming monster. It takes time and dedication to get it right. We become absorbed by the task. Builders and tradespeople don't see it that way. Yours is just one job on a continuum. They have to live with delays and derailment—hold-ups in council approval, objections from neighbours, difficulties in finding tradespeople at the right time, materials shortages, owners who get cold feet and pull out at the last minute.

They always have an eye on the next few jobs down the line. They need alternatives somewhere in the background which they can pull into line to fill the gaps. The reality of this difficult situation leads to one of the great sources of conflict between builders and owners: delay.

The builder has key objectives—beachheads to secure with the owner. Some are obvious: getting a signed contract and getting a deposit on the job. Others can come as a surprise to home owners and investors. For example, the builder needs to take charge of the site. At the earliest opportunity, the builder will move on to the job site, stack a pile of materials and dig a hole. Then the builder has control of the site against all comers. The job is secure.

I have heard many stories where the builder disappears at this point. Having secured this job, his interest moves to securing the next job. So the builder is off somewhere chasing other owners to get them to commit. This doesn't always happen—sometimes the builder wants to move full steam ahead with the first job, looking towards the schedule of payments. But investors should expect that there will be odd periods like this where the builder is off somewhere else. It might be at the start or it could come later. And, of course, the builder is properly allowed to add time at the end of the planned construction period for any delays beyond the builder's control: poor weather, inability to access the site, unanticipated excavation, delays in obtaining materials, and so on.

My own experience is that financial penalties are no guarantee you will not be left dangling at some point of the job. But you should nevertheless ensure your contract provides for a **financial sanction** ('liquidated damages') against the builder for finishing the work after the desired contractual deadline. Give your solicitor, architect or designer clear instructions to have a daily rate of interest for time overruns included in your contract. Don't assume it will automatically be there simply because it is a fair thing.

And it *is* a fair thing. Look in the building contract and you will see a large section dedicated to protecting the builder's financial interests by imposing a penalty on the owner/developer for delay in making progress payments. The builder will be empowered to charge interest on late payment—reflecting the builder's overdraft rate.

It should cut both ways: you should be compensated for delay caused by the builder at a rate of interest which reflects what you are paying for your finance.

Finding a remedy

Each year, around 5000 consumers in New South Wales alone take their (home) builder to a dispute resolution tribunal. It's a figure which hasn't changed much over the last three years. We can assume that these are people who have failed to find an answer through more informal channels. They are the hard core of a much larger problem. While these figures are for residential disputes, not commercial building work, and from only one state, they nevertheless remind us that a very significant number of construction projects fall into the slow and costly legal system.

If your argument with the builder turns into a drawn-out fight, you may consider taking unilateral action to force the builder back to the negotiating table. This tactic is unusually fraught with danger. This is a complex area of law but I would like to give you a few warning lights to guide you before you head off into the dark of conflict.

- You can't simply walk away from the contract—you must **end it formally**, in accordance with the procedure established in the contract. If you sign up a second builder before legally terminating the first one, you might find yourself being sued by both builders.
- It is an easy trap to believe you can **withhold payment** from the builder with impunity. Building contracts and dispute resolution procedures often work differently to the way you think might be fair. In accordance with the contract, you might legally be obliged to pay the builder what he is due *before* taking the matter to the relevant tribunal or arbitration hearing.
- You might not be able to lawfully lock the builder out of the site until the contract is **formally terminated**. Check the contract wording *and* seek expert legal advice before you interrupt the normal flow of the construction process. It does not matter that there might be some shoddy building work which needs to be remedied—that's what the rectification period (set out in the contract) is all about. Building disputes are complex and procedures must be followed or, amazingly, you could find that *you* become the defaulting party.
- The smart developer is friendly with the builder but never casual. The builder is not your enemy, but construction work is subject to pressure from a host of sources. Find a lawyer who is an expert in building contracts and protect yourself and your project.

Summary

Your strategies for selecting and engaging builders and tradespeople should include these matters:

- Choose only licensed builders and tradespeople and check that their insurances and licences are up to date.
- Obtain expert legal advice on the contract and on any steps you take to assert your rights once the contract has commenced.
- Have your lawyer negotiate the contract to protect your position. In particular, include a penalty for delay by the builder.
- Get all variations to the job noted in writing—signed, dated and, preferably, costed.
- Know where to turn for your remedies.

Section III

MONEY AND RISK

10

What will it cost me?

You need deep pockets when you set out to transform an investment property. They have to be deep if they're going to hold all the bills. No one will give you a reliable all-up figure for your project. The only sure thing is that the total bill will exceed all estimates.

Development costs

There will be costs for many things from a host of agencies and experts. It is essential to plan a proper budget and obtain quotes so you are in a position to cost the project in advance. See Table 10.1 for a list of costs.

Table 10.1 Development costs

Who wants to be paid?	What for?
Professional experts	• Solicitor—legal services • Accountant—accountancy and tax advice • Surveyor • Architect or designer • Town planning consultant • Engineers—structural, hydraulic, other
Council	• Lodgment fees on your multiple applications • 'Contributions'—such as car parking, landscaping, kerbing, driveways and gutters, environmental levies • Road construction (where relevant)

Table 10.1 continued

Who wants to be paid?	What for?
Utilities	Fees for connection of services to the new lots or new dwellings: • water • sewerage • electricity • gas • telephone
State treasury	Stamp duty: • if property will be transferred (perhaps to consolidate the legal title to the site into a new ownership, such as a company name) • mortgage
State land registration authority	Registration fees for a range of matters including: • mortgage • any transfer of ownership • subdivision plan • strata plan • issue of new titles • conversion of title
Garden landscaper	Fee for landscaping site
Builder	• Construction costs • Insurances
Real estate agent	• Commission on sale or rental of property • Advertising expenses
Other	• Fencing • Cleaning • Rubbish removal • Painting
The Tax Office	• Capital gains tax—on sale or disposal of property (unless it is your primary residence) • Income tax on rent

Illustration of project costs

In many ways, it is almost pointless trying to put dollar figures on the costs of a construction project. Still, I find that a guide—no matter how rough—is better than nothing when starting out. Short of actually engaging the experts, it can be difficult to get the information to do those first back-of-the-envelope calculations. So here are some figures for a particular project—however, don't extrapolate too far from them.

For a modest three-townhouse subdivision in an inexpensive area, as well as the land purchase cost (say, $200 000), add any cost of levelling the site or demolition of existing structures and construction/landscaping for the new development. Construction costs are $600 000 and the townhouses will sell for around $350 000 each.

Development application lodgment fee for townhouses	$2 800
Development application lodgment fee for subdivision/boundary readjustment	$300
Council fees for construction inspections, etc.	$2 000
Builders insurance @ $4000 per lot	$12 000
Council contributions @ $1430 per lot	$4 300
Council fee for tapping the water main to plumbing	$900
Town planning consultant	$3 000
Surveyor	$2 500
Legals (solicitor, registering plan, etc.)	$2 000
Site costs (water supply, sewerage, drainage, electrics, access)	$17 000
Total	*$46 800*

You can expect to pay up to two to three times this amount in more expensive or more complicated areas. Add to the bill anything your accountant and/or solicitor might charge for tax advice or for setting up a company structure (if you choose to proceed in that way). This could be a further $2000–$10 000. Then estimate the rest from the listed points above.

The end result is a 'per lot' cost—a figure you will carry with you as a reference point throughout the process.

There are three areas worth a look now:

- stamp duty on the transfer and mortgage;
- tax; and
- financing the deal.

Stamp duty on transfer

This is the stamp duty (state/territory government tax) you will pay on the transfer (sale or purchase) of real estate for a home or as an investment. You might be able to pay less than shown in this table if you are eligible for a government concession scheme—generally for first-home buyers or, in some cases, those purchasing property of low value. These figures are for investors, not home buyers, who may be entitled to various concessional rates. For information on concessions go to the relevant state and territory websites listed at the end of the book.

Table 10.2 State/territory stamp duty on transfer of property

Price	ACT	NSW	NT	Qld	SA	Tas	Vic	WA
$75 000	1500	1203	1941	1663	1955	1675	1600	1725
$100 000	2000	1990	2750	2350	2830	2425	2200	2530
$125 000	2875	2865	3641	3163	3830	3175	3160	3718
$150 000	3750	3740	4613	3975	4830	3925	4660	4905
$175 000	4625	4615	5666	4788	5830	4800	6160	6093
$200 000	5500	5490	6800	5600	6830	5675	7660	7280
$225 000	6500	6365	8016	6413	7893	6550	9160	8468
$250 000	7500	7240	9313	7225	8955	7550	10 660	9655
$275 000	8500	8115	10 691	8100	10 143	8550	12 160	11 130
$300 000	9500	8990	12 150	8975	11 330	9550	13 660	12 605
$325 000	10 875	10 115	13 691	9850	12 580	10 550	15 160	14 080
$350 000	12 250	11 240	15 313	10 725	13 830	11 550	16 660	15 555
$375 000	13 625	12 365	17 016	11 600	15 080	12 550	18 160	17 030
$400 000	15 000	13 490	18 800	12 475	16 330	13 550	19 660	18 505
$425 000	16 375	14 615	20 666	13 350	17 580	14 550	21 160	19 980
$450 000	17 750	15 740	22 613	14 225	18 830	15 550	22 660	21 455
$475 000	19 125	16 865	24 641	15 100	20 080	16 550	24 160	22 930
$500 000	20 500	17 990	26 750	15 975	21 330	17 550	25 660	24 405
$525 000	21 938	19 115	28 350	16 913	22 705	18 550	27 160	25 980
$550 000	23 375	20 240	29 700	17 850	24 080	19 550	28 660	27 555
$575 000	24 813	21 365	31 050	18 788	25 455	20 550	30 160	29 130
$600 000	26 250	22 490	32 400	19 725	26 830	21 550	31 660	30 705
$625 000	27 688	23 615	33 750	20 663	28 205	22 550	33 160	32 280
$650 000	29 125	24 740	35 100	21 600	29 580	23 550	34 660	33 855
$675 000	30 563	25 865	36 450	22 538	30 955	24 550	36 160	35 430
$700 000	32 000	26 990	37 800	23 475	32 330	25 550	37 660	37 005
$800 000	37 750	31 490	43 200	27 225	37 830	29 550	43 660	43 305

Price	ACT	NSW	NT	Qld	SA	Tas	Vic	WA
$800 000	37 750	31 490	43 200	27 225	37 830	29 550	43 660	43 305
$900 000	43 500	35 990	48 600	30 975	43 330	33 550	49 500	49 605
$1 000 000	49 250	40 490	54 000	34 725	48 830	37 550	55 000	55 905
$1 500 000	83 000	67 990	81 000	53 475	76 330	57 550	82 500	87 405
$2 000 000	116 750	95 490	108 000	72 225	103 830	77 550	110 000	118 905
$3 000 000	184 250	150 490	162 000	109 720	158 830	117 550	165 000	181 905

Rounded to nearest dollar

Stamp duty on mortgages

For information on concessions, go to the relevant websites listed at the end of the book. There is no mortgage stamp duty in the ACT or Northern Territory.

Table 10.3 State/territory stamp duty on mortgages

Mortgage	NSW	Queensland	SA	Tasmania	Victoria	WA
$50 000	141	200	208	165	164	148
$100 000	341	400	433	340	364	348
$150 000	541	600	658	515	564	548
$200 000	741	800	883	690	764	748
$250 000	941	1000	1108	865	964	948
$300 000	1141	1200	1333	1040	1164	1148
$350 000	1341	1400	1558	1215	1364	1348
$400 000	1541	1600	1783	1390	1564	1548
$450 000	1741	1800	2008	1565	1764	1748
$500 000	1941	2000	2233	1740	1964	1948
$550 000	2141	2200	2458	1915	2164	2148
$600 000	2341	2400	2683	2090	2364	2348
$650 000	2541	2600	2908	2265	2564	2548
$700 000	2741	2800	3133	2440	2764	2748
$750 000	2941	3000	3358	2615	2964	2948
$800 000	3141	3200	3583	2790	3164	3148
$850 000	3341	3400	3808	2965	3364	3348
$900 000	3541	3600	4033	3140	3564	3548
$950 000	3741	3800	4258	3315	3764	3748
$1 000 000	3941	4000	4483	3490	3964	3948
$1 500 000	5941	6000	6733	5240	5964	5948
$2 000 000	7941	8000	8983	6990	7964	7948
$3 000 000	11 941	12 000	13 483	10 490	11 964	11 948

Rounded to nearest dollar

It soon adds up. However, you may be able to borrow the stamp duty (and other expenses) as part of your overall property loan.

Tax: Get in tune with it

When a property is turned to investment purposes, you are switching on the tax tap—income and capital gains become assessable and many (but not all) expenses become deductible. Further, some expenses will be deductible in the year they were incurred (so you get the tax benefit reasonably quickly), some over time via depreciation, while other costs will only come back to you when you sell or otherwise dispose of the property (as part of the capital gains tax calculation). How you handle the tax implications of your project will largely determine whether you come out ahead or with the seat out of your pants barely intact. It's vital to get the tax situation right.

Clearly you need to know exactly what work you do and which things you buy are entitled to a tax concession. There's depreciation of the building itself, as well as many of the things within it, so get hold of a current depreciation list from your accountant. Other matters—travel expenses to the site, marketing costs and so on—might simply be tax deductible. For more information, purchase a copy of the most recent *Australian Master Tax Guide* (published by CCH).

The most important thing is to get up-to-date information, as these things have a habit of changing. I would, however, like to raise a few key points to remind you what to discuss with your tax advisers. Two of these areas will have an enormous taxation impact on you and your project: capital gains tax (CGT) and the goods and services tax (GST).

Capital Gains Tax

Although CGT tax is only paid at the end—as part of your next tax assessment once you have sold or otherwise disposed of your property—critical elements take place right at the start when you purchase the property. Don't mess them up.

Capital Gains Tax is a wealth tax raised by the federal government on property acquired on or after 20 September 1985. Generally, your principal place of residence is exempt, as is any property acquired before that date. If you sell or dispose of an investment property for more money than it cost you there may be a liability to pay tax on the gain. For example, if you purchased a property for $300 000 and sold it three years later for $400 000, the nominal capital gain would be $100 000 and this would be added to your income for tax purposes.

Fortunately, it is not this basic in application and the tax burden can be minimised. For property purchased or acquired on or after 21 September 1999, capital gains tax is calculated in this way: you add 50 per cent of the *net capital gain* to your income for tax assessment purposes. Your marginal income tax rate determines how much tax you will have to pay. The maximum rate is 24.25 per cent—half the highest marginal tax rate of 48.5 per cent (which includes the Medicare levy).

Expenses which are deducted to arrive at the net gain include:

- capital costs of the purchase: stamp duty on the transfer, solicitor's or conveyancer's fees and disbursements on the conveyancing;
- capital costs of selling: real estate agent's fees and commission, legal expenses, etc.;
- improvements: building costs for improvements, minus any tax benefit you have already claimed such as depreciation.

Under the discount method of calculating CGT, there is no allowance for the effects of inflation on reducing the value of the money you have spent. Note that the 50 per cent discount is only available to an individual or a trust—a company does not get it. This may affect your decision to own your investment property via a company structure and is something to discuss with your accountant and advisers prior to commencement of work.

If, as an individual or trust, you sell or dispose of the property too soon—within twelve months of purchasing or acquiring it—you miss out on the 50 per cent discount. This means your net capital gain will be taxed in full at whatever marginal income tax rate you are paying—up to 48.5 per cent at the top end of the scale. This may affect your strategy as to when to buy and when to sell.

Where property was purchased or acquired on or before 20 September 1985, you have an alternative method of capital gains tax calculation open to you which you might want to use. Under this older method, inflation is taken into account in calculating the real cost of having owned the property (provided you have owned it for at least twelve months). All expenses are indexed to the cost of living. The government, however, has frozen the indexation principle at 20 September 1999—after that date, no inflation will be taken into account on your expenses. So their value to you will fall away over time. Another principle which you might have heard of—averaging of capital gains over a number of years to get a fairer figure for tax—ceased back in the 1999/2000 financial year.

Timing is important. Obviously you want to own the property for long enough to get the benefit of the concession. But there's more to consider. As you can see, the capital gain is added to your income for income tax assessment purposes—it doesn't sit out there somewhere on its own. And your marginal rate of income tax determines how much tax you will pay.

For example, if you have been slaughtered on the stock market and have a capital loss situation it might be a convenient financial year to sell an asset of real estate which has improved in value, thereby applying the capital loss against the gain. Then again, if you have retired or are about to retire, you should seek expert advice on the timing of an asset sale and its interaction with retirement payouts. There are a number of strategies to discuss with your accountant so that you take charge of your tax situation rather than get blown around by fate and poor choices.

Good records are essential if you are to avoid trouble yet also get your full entitlement to deductions. By law, you are required to keep records of all matters about your capital gain (or loss) for five years after you have sold or disposed of the property.

Improvements

Your property may in fact comprise a number of different assets which will each require its own capital gains tax calculation—for example, where there are several buildings on the land. If, when you sell or otherwise dispose of the property, you and the purchaser agree on an allocation of the sale price in the contract between the various assets, the taxation commissioner will accept that allocation for CGT purposes. Failing this agreement, you can still make your own apportionment, provided it is reasonable and based on market values. It is wise to get the assets valued by a registered valuer.

The rules are highly technical and deal with such situations as building now on land which was acquired before CGT came into force—part of the value is caught by the tax, part may be exempt; or where two blocks of land (one acquired pre-CGT, the other post-CGT) are amalgamated into one title. These are matters for discussion with your advisers.

Will you be paying too much tax?

Income tax withholding variation

You're going to incur a large amount in tax deductions during the course of your development. However, you won't see the financial benefit of this until you have lodged your tax return and received a cheque back from the Tax Office or otherwise enjoyed the reduction in tax you have to pay. You're carrying the load for months or even years!

But there is a part of the taxation legislation which lets you lower the rate of tax withheld from your income *in advance* where you know your tax deductions that financial year will leave the Tax Office having to issue you with a refund. This means that you will get the tax benefit week by week.

The strategy is to apply to the Tax Office for a variation in the rate of tax withheld from your salary. There are some things you should be aware of, however:

- You must apply each year—each variation ends on 30 June.
- You still have to get the figures right—the mere fact the Tax Office approves your variation application does not mean it agrees with your figures. Your position may well be adjusted when your tax return is assessed.

- You may be prosecuted and fined if you have provided false and misleading information.
- You must advise the Tax Office of any change in your circumstances that will affect the variation (e.g. you sell the relevant property).
- All your tax affairs must be up to date before your application will be approved.
- You can apply online.

For further information, or to get a paper application form, phone 1300 360 221 or email ITWvariation@ato.gov.au.

Paying an extra year's interest in advance

You might also wish to consider the strategy of paying an extra year's interest on your business or investment borrowings during the current financial year—that is, up to a total of two years' interest in the one twelve-month period. You can get a tax deduction for up to twelve months' interest paid in advance. You might want to take advantage of this opening if you are facing immediate difficulties and could really do with maximising your business deductions in the current year. Again, seek expert advice before acting.

ABN and GST

Since 1 July 2000, Australia has had the goods and services tax (GST). GST is added to most of the goods and services you will need for your project—such as professional fees from your consultants and builders, construction materials, sales agent's commission, advertising—and, at the other end, GST must be included in the sales price of new residential premises (for example, those three new townhouses you have built).

Accordingly, you should seek expert advice from your accountant about applying for an Australian Business Number (ABN) and registration for GST purposes. The ABN is an identification number for your business dealings with the Tax Office—you must be carrying on a business for profit, not merely as a hobby. Registration for GST puts you in the pipeline so that you can recover the

GST you pay for goods and services used by your business enterprise (input tax credits). And you must account to the tax office for the GST applied to what you sell.

Generally speaking, the Tax Office will regard larger development projects as an 'enterprise' for which you must get an ABN and register for GST. This is true even if the project will just be a one-off. (When the project has been completed and the property or properties sold, you can deregister if you wish.)

It is important that you get your registration in the right name or names. If you use a company or run the project under your own name, that is simple enough. But if, for example, you are already registered because you run your own business and your partner in the development is not currently registered (perhaps they are an employee or non-working spouse), the Tax Office will look upon the pair of you as a **separate tax entity**. You will be a tax partnership and must register as that partnership *separately* from your own existing business or personal registration.

There are many wrinkles. Note that if you hang on to your property and rent it out, the situation might be different. From that time, if they are residential premises, you cannot claim input tax credits and will not add GST to the rent; if the premises are commercial or industrial, you add GST to the rent and claim back the input tax credits on your expenses. That's because there is a specific exemption for residential rental property (called 'input taxed supplies'). And if your project is a pure greenfields subdivision where you make no improvements to the property (no fences, services, buildings, etc.), when you sell it might be regarded as the disposal of a capital asset with no obligation to register for ABN/GST.

Did you own the property prior to 1 July 2000? If so, you may wish to take advantage of a transitional tax arrangement for GST called the margin scheme.

The margin scheme

When the time comes to sell your investment property, you should seek expert advice on making the GST calculation, as this tax must be included in the price for which the property is sold. Transitional arrangements—called the margin scheme—can reduce the amount of tax and therefore help you sell your property for a lower overall price. This can give you a competitive advantage in the marketplace.

It's your choice, as vendor, whether to simply add the 10 per cent tax or to use the margin method, and there are two ways of applying the margin method: by consideration or valuation. If you choose the 'consideration' margin method, you calculate GST on the difference in the price you paid for the property (pre-July 2000) and what you sold it for—a straight subtraction of one price from another. Alternatively, if you choose the valuation margin method you must get your property valued as at the relevant date (usually 1 July 2000) and subtract that figure (not your original purchase price) from the sale price.

Then there are five different ways of making your property valuation. You don't include costs (e.g. conveyancing fees) or stamp duty, but something as simple as an adjustment of rates between vendor and purchaser—if it adds to the sale price—will be included in the figure against which tax is calculated. It really is a matter for your accountant's advice.

Whichever way you do it, the purchaser has no control over the matter—the purchaser can't even claim an input tax credit for the GST included in the price.

Importantly, you must have evidence *at the time of sale* that you were using the margin method to apply GST to your property. Otherwise the Tax Office might assume you did not make this choice and will want to be paid the full 10 per cent. The necessary evidence will be a reference to the application of the margin scheme in the contract of sale, in a letter of instruction to your conveyancer, in a company or trust minute or in a file note. According to the Tax Office:

> The particulars should sufficiently identify the real property that is the subject of the supply, for example, a project lot number, certain lots on a particular estate, or land contained in a specified contract. Your course of conduct or pattern of dealing with sales of real property may also provide evidence of your choice to apply the margin scheme.

It's a critical step.

For more information, contact the Tax Office or go to its website. You could also phone the Business Infoline on 13 28 66 or obtain *A Fax from Tax* on 13 28 60.

There are a number of GST traps for the unwary. For example, a residential property will be classified as 'new' when it is finally sold, despite having been held by you and rented out for a number of years (after five years, it is no longer considered 'new'). And if you take an old home on a large block and build some units in the backyard, GST must be added to the sale price of the new units but not to the existing house when sold. A similar principle applies where you take a block of flats on one title and strata title them for individual sale. Under more recent Tax Office rulings, there is no GST added to their price. This gives the seller a price advantage in the marketplace which they can exploit.

These are complex matters, and the rules have a habit of changing—clearly you should design your project and its timing after detailed discussions with your tax advisers.

If you want to do some reading on the subject, you can pick up brochures from the Tax Office, phone them on 13 28 66 or go to their website at www.ato.gov.au. You register for an ABN and GST with the Tax Office.

Financing the project

How do you intend paying for your development? Will you:

- pay cash;
- work with a partner who pays cash;
- borrow everything against the property and the development consent;
- use your home (and/or other property) equity to assist as part-security for the loan (back in March 2003 home equity loans accounted for 14 per cent of all housing loans—Australians are really getting into this source of finance);
- get the interest capitalised and borrow it up-front;
- use a construction loan—secured against the ongoing improvement in value of the property;

- use a line of credit on your home loan or an investment loan;
- redraw on the current loan—if you're ahead in your repayments;
- seek finance from non-conforming lenders?

Your bank, or other lender, is principally interested in four things:

- whether you can provide sufficient security for the loan;
- whether you can afford the repayments;
- how to accurately value the changing worth of the property as work progresses; and
- whether you will go elsewhere for your money.

There is no magic to any of this. No longer does an investor have to head down dark alleys to find the finance necessary for his or her development project. Start with your own bank, building society or credit union and move further afield to see who offers you the best deal. In assessing the deals, bear the following in mind:

- **How much security do they want?** Will the lender require a mortgage over your home as well as over your investment property (development site)? Less is better. If you can keep one property unencumbered by mortgage, you can always seek to borrow against it later if you are short of cash. If everything you own is tied up with the one lender, and it loses confidence in you, you will find the financial climate can turn very frosty.

  Personal guarantees are often required by the lender. This means you are placing all your assets on the line should things go bad, not just your real estate. Be wary, however, of giving the lender personal guarantees from other members of your family. The lender may ask you about their financial circumstances as part of a fishing expedition to see where further guarantees or security might be lurking. But these wider family guarantees have a nasty habit of wrecking families and ending up in the courts. Don't do it.

  If you feel you have to drag in dad or mum to back you up or the deal will not get the go-ahead, get them separate legal advisers and ensure the lender agrees—in the documents—to limit their exposure. For example, make their guarantee limited to, say, a maximum of $50 000. And the terms should be amended so that the lender can't go after your family until they have exhausted the proceeds of sale of your property (or properties) and all your personal assets. Put mum and dad at the end of the line. Again, however, I say don't do it.

✓ *Tip:* Keep some cash or assets where your financier can't quickly freeze them. It's the only way you can finance your living expenses and survive your negotiations when the shutters come down.

- **What interest rate will they charge?** Don't be surprised to find a range of interest rates on offer. But which is the best rate? One useful tool is the **comparison rate** (see the section on *Using the comparison rate for different loans*, below). If you have plenty of equity to put into the deal as security but are short on cashflow, you might want to discuss borrowing the interest as well as the principal of the loan. Clearly this will cost you more. But if you are confident the builder can do the job on time and that the market is desperate to buy what you are selling, then it is a strategy (albeit a dangerous one) worth serious consideration. It is not something to be entered into lightly or simply because the lender strongly suggests it.
- **What fees do they want?** These can include an initial or establishment fee for investigating the deal and setting up the documentation, plus ongoing fees and charges (such as a monthly account-keeping fee). Ask about penalties and how you incur them.
- **How flexible and supportive are they?** After discussing the amount you want to borrow, simply ask the financier how they can help you out if you are faced with unplanned expenses—such as unexpected site costs or engineering work. Try not to get into a finance arrangement with a lender who just wants to stick to the rules of the initial deal and who cannot be flexible enough to adjust to changing circumstances.
- **How will the money be dealt out and by whom?** Lenders have their own standard ways of doling out the money as the

development progresses. Typically, payments relate to the completion of stages of acquisition and construction. Be clear on the arrangements and the schedule. Discuss the requirements with your builder before you commit—you don't want to be caught between the builder's demands and the lender's cautious vested interests with no cash in hand. Ensure that the lender's progress payments schedule lines up precisely with the builder's progress payments schedule as written in the contract.

- **How much will they lend me?** As a general rule, banks and most other lending institutions are more cautious when lending for development than for a simple home or investment property purchase. Even then, however, we have seen the remarkable phenomenon of banks refusing to provide a mortgage over apartments in some of the overheated and overcrowded CBD and inner-city markets in 2002–03—particularly small studio apartments. The risk to the lender of over-exposure was seen to be too high.

  As a guide, you can expect your bank to lend you 70 per cent of what you require for the project—you'll have to put the other 30 per cent on the table. But here we're talking about a mortgage at the most basic interest rate available. Lenders shake their head at you when you ask for 'more please'. For some reason, it just can't be done.

  However, the lender will walk you over to the '**secondary mortgage market**' corner of their office then put another hat on his or her head. This is the hat labelled '**mezzanine finance**'. Mezzanine finance is a second tier of lending, typically offered by high-net-worth individuals or by financial institutions that provide basic home and investment mortgages. Under the mezzanine finance hat, the lender can offer you as much as 90 per cent of what you require—thereby limiting the amount of equity you have to put into the deal—albeit at a higher interest rate. Clearly this is a case of the institution getting a higher financial reward for taking on board a higher level of risk. Deals vary, so you have to shop around more extensively than for a simple property investment loan.

  Mezzanine debt is a rapidly expanding subset of the lending sector in Australia. In part, this is because we are still enmeshed in our love affair with property, but the rise also has its genesis in the collapse of share values and the flood of investors' money into fixed-interest investments with financial institutions early in the 2000s. It's like the dairy cow who is busting to be connected to the milking machine—it's a relief. One of the drivers of mezzanine finance is an imperative to offload large amounts of deposited cash into profitable projects. And so the institutions are more willing to accept higher levels of risk.

Investors working on a number of properties like using mezzanine debt, despite the additional cost, because it allows them to spread their pile of equity around. They can have more than one project on the go at any one time, rather than putting up 30 per cent of the cost of each development. As such, it is a tool for managing your capital and outgoings, particularly in a rising property market. It also helps a person manage his or her risk by enabling more than one project to proceed simultaneously. For example, it might turn out to be easier to sell the units at Cremorne rather than blocks in the land subdivision at Blackheath. As an investor, you can avoid having all your hopes pinned on a single site.

Of course, that is not a luxury we can all afford! If you're reading this book, it's likely you are looking to your first true property development project—or perhaps you're on to your second but were not completely happy with the way the first one went. For first-timers, all the eggs are in one basket.

Obviously the more equity you put into the financing package the lower your ongoing repayment commitments will be, and the less hassle and interference you should get from your lending institution. Interestingly, despite the hype surrounding mezzanine finance, not everyone is enamoured of it. According to a recent survey of small investors (by the consultancy Ashe Morgan Winthrop), only 49 per cent were willing to utilise mezzanine finance and borrow more than 70 per cent of the development requirements. Many other small investors remain cautious of the higher debt/higher interest rate approach. After all, despite the cute name for it, when it all boils down you are simply highly gearing your investment—which is dangerous at any time but all the more so where the property market is falling or even just stumbling.

Using the comparison rate for different loans

With several thousand property loans on offer in the marketplace, it has become difficult to ensure you are getting the right deal for your purpose. The introduction of 'honeymoon' rates—where the borrower pays a lower interest rate for the first six or twelve months of the loan—allowed financial institutions to advertise their deals highlighting the very low initial rate rather than the rate to which the loan would rise when the honeymoon was over. And some loans had cheap or no fees while others cost hundreds of dollars to set up and run.

The task of making a comparison became easier when financial commentators and analysts began assessing loan products using an average annualised percentage rate (AAPR)—a single interest rate figure which bundled the main fees and interest rate factors, including the benefit of a honeymoon period. There were a number of different ways of doing this, and the finance industry was critical that some methods punished one product ahead of another.

Eventually the lead was taken by the Consumer Affairs Ministers, who decided to set a standard way of making the comparison and entrenching this in legislation. The Queensland government was the first to pass this law, amending the Consumer Credit Code back in April 2002. Other states and territories followed, and the law came into force from 1 July 2003. From this date, all mortgage lenders and finance brokers in Australia must state the comparison rate when advertising their fixed-term consumer credit loans using an annual percentage rate.

It is important to know that, while the comparison rate is convenient, it is not a perfect or complete tool. The rate is calculated using a set of standard parameters for relevant loans—for a mortgage, it is a 25-year term with a principal sum of $150 000. So the rate will not be accurate if you are looking at a $400 000 loan or a 30-year term, for example. To deal with this, credit providers must display and make available to consumers copies of a schedule of comparison rates so you can do the comparison on the parameters you want. Note also that some costs will not be included in the rate. (See Table 10.4 on page 176.)

Clearly, all investors must check the loan documents for these other fees and charges. They won't be too hard to find—although the way they are presented does not always make them easy to understand.

You can also go to the website of Cannex (www.cannex.com.au), where the comparison rates for a large number of loan products are presented. The ANZ Bank website, among others (see www.anz.com.au), has a comparison rate calculator which will take different terms and amounts. A mortgage broker will do this for you, too.

Why use a registered valuer?

For your finance application, you will need a valuation of the property. It is easy and cheap to get a real estate agent to provide this. They can look at the land, at your council-approved plans and at the finished work and give you an estimate of value which is often all your financier will require.

But this is not always the best approach—sometimes you should use a registered valuer instead. Why? Because a court of law will accept their valuation but not generally the valuation provided by a real estate agent. This is important if, for example:

- you get into a fight with the Tax Office over depreciation or capital gains tax;
- you are developing the site in partnership with others and one of you gets fed up (or dies) and an apportionment must be made;
- you split from your spouse;
- you want precise insurance cover—you don't want to pay too much premium, yet you want to be absolutely covered against loss;
- you are putting the development to auction and want to set a reserve price which you can justify to anyone at any time.

A written valuation report from a licensed valuer can also be useful if your financier closes the tap and won't advance any more money. If you can establish a higher value for your project than is

Table 10.4 Advertising of interest rates—mandatory use of a comparison rate

What the comparison rate includes	What it does not include
Application fees	Fees for redrawing money
The interest rate	Penalties for early repayment of the loan
Any 'honeymoon' or introductory interest rate	Any other fees for *features* of the loan
Known ongoing fees and charges for running the loan (e.g. monthly service fees)	The value to you of personal reasons for using a particular financial institution: a relationship, convenience of location, etc.
	Fees which cannot be ascertained at the start of the loan, and fees which are dependent on some other action (e.g. overdue payment)
	Government charges and fees (e.g. stamp duty)
	The features of the loan: redraw, link to other accounts and products (e.g. 100 per cent offset accounts, credit cards, insurance arrangements)
	Interest-only loans, credit cards, line-of-credit and business loans

currently on the table, you might just be able to get your finance extended.

At the moment, you might not think you will end up in anything like these situations but, when everything hits the fan, you'll be glad you've got a rock-solid valuation report you can throw on someone's desk.

A registered valuer determines the worth of your development property by reference to past sales and/or rental figures for the area and for similar properties in the light of prevailing economic trends. The valuer will report on the site and the condition of any improvements (buildings, pool, quality, state of repair, etc.). Supporting materials are provided in the written valuation report which you receive. Valuers are bound to act independently, bowing to no one's vested interest.

Get a quote before you commission the valuer. If the property is worth less than $500 000 and there are no wrinkles or complexities, you can expect to pay from a few hundred dollars to something like $600 for the report. The price goes up from there.

Summary

- You'll be paying an army of people—work out the costs in advance and calculate a rough 'per lot' figure to guide you through the development process.
- There will be sizeable payments to council (especially for contributions), for stamp duty and estate agents (commissions and promotion expenses).
- You may wish to borrow some of these expenses as part of your financing.
- Find a good tax accountant and design your project with tax considerations in mind. In particular, plan for your CGT and GST liabilities and responsibilities. Decide whether you should proceed with the project in your name or set up a company structure.
- Seek advice on financial strategies including whether to apply for a variation in your income tax withholding rate; consider the pre-payment of interest by 30 June.
- Find a financier who is supportive and comfortable with what you intend doing. They should be experienced in financing development work and comfortable with the ups and downs of development.
- Prepare a comprehensive back-up plan to save your skin (see Chapter 11).
- Check the comparative rate of various loan options and get the features you want.
- Use a registered valuer for finance and CGT reasons.

11

Getting out of trouble

The reality is that sometimes a property improvement scheme goes bad and it's hard to know what to do about it. You can give up the struggle (and possibly have to sell at a loss) or you can fight on. But maybe you've already reached the wall and there is nowhere left to turn. What then?

Back-up strategies

What will your disaster back-up plan look like? Consider these five strategies:

- **Rent it out.** If you intended selling the property or properties, but it's not working out, have your figures and plans ready for finding tenants until the market improves. If you intended keeping the properties and renting, but can't get the tenants, you will need a scheme for bailing out and selling the properties.

  Let's assume you are subdividing a house into two villas or units and converting them to strata/unit title for individual sale. First you do your figures on the development and the sale:

Estimated sale price (total)		$1 000 000
Less		
Purchase price	$200 000	
Development costs	$450 000	

Interest on finance	$120 000	
Sales commissions and marketing	$35 000	
Total costs	$805 000	$805 000
Profit before tax		**$195 000**

That's the plan. But what if the market falls? If prices drop by 20 per cent, you will *lose* on the scheme. And that's leaving aside the cost of your time—which will be unpaid now.

What will you do? Consider renting out the two villas/units until the sales market picks up again. If the property is in a good location, you can expect to regain the missing $200 000 by selling in a few years' time (if history is anything to go by).

Let's say your minimum holding cost of finance, rates, insurance, managing agent's commission and maintenance (lawns, etc.) is $60 000 per year.

Holding cost	$60 000
Per unit	$30 000
Or, per week	$577
Agent's estimate of achievable weekly rent	$500
Shortfall	$77 per week per unit

Can you carry this expense of $154 per week to hold the property until the sales market improves? Bear in mind that this loss should be tax deductible.

But if the agent tells you the likely rent would only be $400 per week, you'd be facing a weekly burden of $354 to defer selling. That's a big difference.

- **Find a developer to buy you out**. If you end up fighting your builder—and this is always on the cards—construction work will likely cease. Inevitably, rain and, mysteriously, a freak hail storm will ruin 20 per cent of the building materials. But you have already sussed out some alternatives, including back-up builders and/or contact details for a number of investors or developers who might be prepared to buy the mess off you in its *unfinished* state. Local estate agents will help you with names and phone numbers, or you could go to local new property open days and chat with the developers. Open some channels of communication which you might want to use in dire circumstances.

Swap shop

The Rogerson family—two generations—worked in property in the eastern suburbs of Sydney. They dealt with a fairly sophisticated style of customer and had marketing tactics to suit. And they had become very successful. One of the children was now a real estate agent and was doing fine at that too.

Having trawled their local patch for deals, they were tempted to start a project in Sydney's western suburbs. It was a long way from their territory but they felt they knew the Sydney market well and were comfortably confident. They purchased a large stretch of land from a grazier, with the intention of subdividing it to create house lots. The zoning permitted this use and the deal looked straightforward. Given their background, there was certainly no difficulty in raising the finance.

Six months later, however, things had ground to a halt. They were in litigation with the council over conditions placed on consent and they were battling various trades and unions. The site was muddy trench warfare on the Western Front. The deal was rapidly turning into a disaster.

Meanwhile, in another part of town, there was a property developer named Ian who was also in a tight spot. He specialised in small office redevelopments outside the CBD. But he had been tempted by the bright lights of the big city and was enmeshed in a catastrophe of his own.

Ian had acquired a number of houses and factories and was busily turning them into a shopping centre towards the east of the city—new territory for him. The building was basically finished, but he was getting little interest from prospective tenants. The bank was knocking at the door and demanding evidence that cash was on its way to pull the loan back into line. Some signed leases would do the trick but he only had around a third of the shops let—and mostly to small fry. Now his major tenant—a supermarket—was getting uneasy. Everyone was losing confidence in the developer, and therefore in the site. No one wanted to be tied to a shopping centre with a whiff of collapse in the air.

Both investors had the same solicitor. One day they found themselves face to face in the solicitor's waiting room with time to kill. They had seen each other over the years and would give a small nod of recognition, but they knew little of each other's business.

That day they spoke openly about the trials and tribulations of guiding projects through council and getting them built. Soon it became apparent they were both on the ropes over their current properties. When Ian heard about the stalled subdivision in the western suburbs, he offered all sorts of helpful advice. After all, this was his area and he knew how to handle builders and councils. And Sam Rogerson recognised the issues surrounding the filling of a shopping centre with quality tenants in the eastern suburbs. His family had done it before and had all the right contacts.

They decided that, although they wouldn't help each other, they were prepared to deal. They swapped projects. There was a cash adjustment, but essentially they took over each other's job.

Things moved rapidly now. Contracts for sale were prepared and exchanged. Within a matter of days, the Rogersons' real estate agent son made a phone call to a contact. That contact inspected the partially completed shopping centre and purchased it from the family on the spot. (The contact knew how to land the major tenants and the centre is now a flourishing and key part of its suburb.) The profit was significant.

Initially, Ian was furious. So much money made on a single phone call! But he had nothing to complain about. He jumped into the subdivision, threw his weight and some cash around, and got it back on track. He knew what he was doing and wasn't intimidated by the necessary work or the tough people he had to deal with. Soon the subdivision was in the hands of estate agents for marketing and the first deposits were placed on home sites. Ian also made a handsome profit.

- **Keep a back-up financier in the wings**. Even though you have your finance sorted out with your primary lender, financial institutions can get the wobbles when a project deviates from the plan. If the cash dries up, it is important to have someone else to turn to who might refinance the construction and pay out your mortgagee. For this, you need an established relationship—preferably one based on successful mutual experience. And it's hard to get someone to put their trust—and money—in you when you have a wild, desperate look in your eyes.
- **Obtain more than one council approval for the property**. You can get both applications moving through council simultaneously—imagine the time this will save later if you can't find a tenant or purchaser. If you are unsure how far your finances will stretch, design **relatively compartmentalised stages** into your development and/or applications. For example, if you are

adding a second dwelling at the back of an existing property, you might design the job into these eight stages:

1 the second dwelling itself;
2 the garage: just use the car space until the garage can be erected;
3 more elaborate landscaping;
4 a swimming pool;
5 cabana and pool room/changing facility;
6 an improved joint laundry (for both dwellings to use);
7 a built-in fireplace: a feature like this will cost $10 000. If designed with staging in mind, you can defer this task and its expense;
8 other improvements to the existing dwelling—for example, constructing a sunroom or adding an ensuite bathroom to the master bedroom. Perhaps you are living there and want to take advantage of having the construction team working on the new dwelling in the backyard by getting them to carry out some work on your home too. If you have to, you can delay or delete this section of the job.

The key issues are:

- Get your designer to draw the plans with staging in mind.
- Obtain council approval for the total project.
- Focus on completing one stage before moving on to the next one (if it is economically and practically feasible to do so). If you have to pull the plug and sell, your property has a number of completed improvements—rather than being a mess of incomplete work-in-progress which is of negative value.

You don't have to construct each and every stage as approved by council. The consent document will state a time limit after which the consent expires and you may have to reapply later if you still want to proceed with a deferred stage. Bear in mind that regulations and community expectations may be different at that later date—subsequent approval cannot be assumed. Still, sometimes we have to cut back on the project and get it sold or earning income.

A bet each way

With an eye to his retirement, Stan figured he would add some commercial property to his residential portfolio. Looking around, he found a builder putting up a set of factory units around a U-shaped road. There were units both inside and outside the U. Here was an opportunity to purchase off the plan.

'I could see they were very basic: just like a big concrete garage with a tin roof and a mezzanine office. Normally I would never buy off the plan, because there is too much that can go wrong with residential construction. But here there was little to mess up so I felt secure.

'It was a very early stage in the development and nothing had been built. I knew this was a time when the developer would be open to accepting a low offer in order to take the pressure off his financing arrangements. Curiously the developer had decided that the units on the way in—along the one-way road—were more valuable and desirable than those on the way out. I did not share this belief and was quite prepared to make my offer on one of these cheaper 'exit' units.

'After the usual haggling, I got the developer down to quite a low price—this would be his first sale. As soon as he agreed, I said: "OK, I'll have the one next to it too!" This took him by surprise, but what could he do? He had to let me have the second one at the same low first-cab-off-the-rank price. I had my bargain.

'It didn't stop there. My strategy was to minimise my *risk* by maximising my options. As part of the deal I got him to put a door between the two factory units (they shared a common wall). This would allow me to market the units to small business tenants and to those who had grown in size and needed the extra space.

'Continuing this theme, I lodged development applications with council for approval to use the properties either for commercial or industrial applications. In fact, one application was for majority commercial/minority industrial use and the second was for majority industrial/minority commercial use. Again, this strategy would expand my marketing options.

'So I got myself into a position where I could find tenants for the units in different market segments based on *size* of the business and *use*.

'In the end, I made only one dud decision (and that because I followed the advice of an "expert"). I decided to differentiate my units from the other identical ones in the U-shaped development by raising the level of finishes. I hoped to attract better tenants, or at least to secure tenants more quickly than my neighbouring owners. So I paid for a classier fit-out for both units.

'As it turned out, I get the same rent as the other factory units with their much more basic fit-outs. I don't know that any tenant is ever completely happy with the fit-out as supplied standard, so they don't want to pay extra for what you've done. I won't make that mistake again!'

Stan's project is a commercial/industrial situation, but we should think in a similar manner about our residential projects. These are marketing decisions with implications for our construction strategies. Consider whether there is any point in seeking more than one consent, more than one design, more than one use. For example, if you are working on a house near a shopping precinct, should you be planning the design and applying to council for both straight residential and mixed residential/commercial/home business occupation use? Decide whether you are targeting a home buyer, a small business operator or someone who wants to work from home—or all three.

- **Find an investment partner**. Your relationship partner is upset. He or she is fed up with you never being home, with your short temper, the endless meetings, the tight financial reins which have strangled your previously enjoyable lifestyle. This type of more active investment strategy can put stress on relationships. We all need a better back-up plan than divorce. Is there a potential equity partner who might come in on the project with you and share the load? Or will you have to get out totally if your relationship is suffering?

There is a saying that 'Napoleon never committed his reserves'. He had faith in his plans but nevertheless kept extra resources nearby should they be needed. Start your Disaster File when everyone is happy and the sky is clear. (By the way, Napoleon lost *badly* at Waterloo. There are no guarantees in war, or with property improvement.)

The smart property investor has his or her alternative strategies in mind at the time the purchase is made. Hopefully you won't need them, but you can't control the economy. It is a clever move to have your alternatives ticking along in the background as you proceed with the main game.

Summary

Prepare your back-up plan.

- If your plan is to own the property and rent it out, also establish the likely sale value.
- If your plan is to sell the property, also establish the likely rent in case you have to keep it.
- Acquire contact details for other investors and developers working in your area—they may be prepared to pick up your partially complete project or become your partner in the deal.
- Figure out what you would have to do to *differentiate* your property from others competing for the same tenants or buyers.
- Consider applying to council for general or multiple consents.
- Consider drafting plans which allow you to stage your project in distinct, affordable pieces.
- Make plans which are realistic given your family situation and relationships. Don't ignore your partner or family—divorce will really mess up your grand vision for financial independence.

12

A final word: Motivation

What's your motivation for doing all this extra, difficult work on your investment property? If it's just to make money I suggest you stick to small-scale projects such as home renovation where keeping a close eye on what happens is a straightforward process and it is relatively easy to steer the project to a positive conclusion.

All the successful medium and larger-scale property investors I've worked with have much more invested in their projects than money and the desire to make more of it. Generally speaking, they love what they do. They are driven to negotiate and they are strangely refreshed by battle.

They are extremely resourceful—there is no problem they can't fix. Often they don't even realise how the problems get solved. It's like they've got a magic wand to wave over troubled waters. They begin as self-assured people and gradually turn into supremely confident leaders.

What they don't realise is that they stand upon the shoulders of a lot of hard-working, responsible people. Some are experts—in accountancy, law, town planning and design—and others are just friends who help out. Why do they do it? In part, it's because they are being paid to do their jobs, and the friends help out of affection and concern. But there's more to it.

Successful property 'transformers' have highly attractive personalities. Some are genuinely charismatic: they draw people to themselves. They can be fun to be with—outrageous, humorous, lively, splashing the cash around liberally. Others may be quieter, but with a brooding intensity that is compelling.

Their strong personalities are a secret of their success. They lie behind these people's ability to keep a lot of balls up in the air at the same time. Increasingly, as the deals roll by, they can feel they are invincible. People want to be involved with them. Unfortunately these strong personality traits can work both ways: they are lovable and they can be harsh.

In short, a need to make money is not enough. Active investing of this kind is an emotional and financial drain. You either need powerful commitment to the project or, as an alternative, a very high disposable income so that you can handle the financial pressures which accompany delay and indecision. You've got to ask yourself if you have the personality for success in working to reshape investment property. Do you attract people? When you go to the shop counter does the person serving you offer to 'go out the back and see if there might still be one in stock', then find what you want *and* offer to gift-wrap it for you?

As this book comes to its close, I would like to reinforce one of its ongoing themes: be charming and influence people. It's the same lesson for the modest investor as for the major developer. You may be dealing with the very same bureaucrats and officials. Everywhere you turn there is the potential to make an ally or an enemy—among councillors, council officers, your consultants and experts, in the community. Usually we don't realise we've got something wrong until we're a long way down a steep track.

In no small measure, that's because we don't always see clearly that we have made an enemy. The smart investor knows that his or her project will excite many people who come across it. Most people like to get a sniff of what they might call 'easy money'. If they think they're going to get a piece of the action, and then miss out, they can be vengeful. This next illustration comes from a large townhouse development, but it serves as a warning to those working on more modest projects where marketing is a critical factor.

Think about how you do your deals and be careful about making any enemies. Will the word go out against your project?

Could local real estate agents be vindictive? Will they be inhospitable should an 'outside' agency enter their turf?

The screwer gets screwed

Opposite a beautiful park sat an old, rundown government building on a huge site. The government, in the classic modern mode of 'sell every capital asset in order to balance the current account', had contributed to its dire state. Of course once the building had fallen into fatal disrepair, who could blame the government for selling it off?

The site was purchased by an inter-state developer who saw the potential of the land for a quality residential subdivision. The blocks at the front would enjoy peerless views over wonderful and exotic parkland. If he made them two-storey, the views would reel in the customers at premium prices.

The developer started getting plans drawn up for a frightening number of villas and townhouses. They were jammed together like cockroaches under a Sydney fridge. The drawings said they had period charm, though this really meant they were straight out of Victorian England in the depths of the Industrial Revolution.

This inter-state developer didn't know anyone locally. His team flew in and got organised with the council and then went searching for an estate agent to handle the all-important marketing. Quickly they found out who were the main quality players in that part of town.

After a succession of business meetings, the estate agent of choice gave its quote for marketing and selling the homes. It worked out at something like 3 per cent of the value of the development. I didn't think this was too bad—the job would be very demanding and would extend over a couple of years.

But the developer's representatives weren't satisfied. Moving to 'second-tier' estate agencies, they wandered further and further afield until, from just over the horizon, they struck a deal with an agent who was prepared to market and sell the homes for 1.5 per cent—half price.

They returned to their agent-of-choice and put the screws on to match the outsider. The job was worth hundreds of thousands of dollars to the agent, but the agent wouldn't budge. Acceptance of the job would require additional staff and substantial resources. It would pull the business away from serving its current stable of good clients. It could be dangerous to the ongoing health of the agency. No, it would only do it for 3 per cent.

The developer walked away. 'You will live to regret this!' they said to each other.

The fringe-dwelling estate agency started into the marketing with gusto but was working in unfamiliar, more up-market territory. A number of problems emerged with the site, including an environmental issue which hit the local papers, and the developer and agent were floundering. Prices for the villas and townhouses were pitched at the top end of the market. Potential purchasers were asked to make a substantial leap of faith.

They didn't leap. They were going to wait and see how the development took shape. And while the agent was working hard to persuade home buyers and investors to commit—it was, all agreed, a fantastic site opposite the park—there was, in a Newtonian physics sense, an 'equal and opposite force' at work. Other estate agents who were positioned closer to the development were cautioning their clients against buying in. After a year or so, only one holding deposit had been taken. And after a while, even this glimmer of hope was withdrawn. The purchaser took his money back and invested elsewhere. This was a body blow to the inter-state developer at a stage of proceedings when things were already looking grim.

You see, that purchaser just happened to be a long-standing client of the estate agent who had held out for his 3 per cent. The agent's advice to his client was to avoid buying an investment property in this development.

Major developers have the muscle to move into an area and run over the top of local businesses. Much of their marketing is aimed entirely elsewhere—overseas and to their own extensive client list. The smaller-scale investor, however, needs local friends and support (or at least a neutral attitude to the project).

Plan how you will keep local estate agents on-side, even when you have signed exclusive marketing arrangements with a sole agent. Local investors put value on the opinions of agents who have helped them establish their property portfolios.

Too close to your property?

What is your motivation for taking the step beyond property investing and into transformation? As you progress with your development, with all its twists, turns, frustrations and success, consider this: how close are you to your project?

The one that got away

Although Harvey had always enjoyed competitive sport, it was not to be his career. Instead of a life of excitement and thrills, he duly went to university, studied hard and became an accountant.

Of course, he prospered. He bought a home, then another, then a holiday home. Then he went searching for bigger and brighter opportunities. Out the back of one of his properties was what he called 'a barren wasteland'. Could it be made more financially productive?

After noting the lack of high-quality sports facilities in his area, Harvey was chatting one day with some professional sports people and hit upon the idea of creating a centre for sports excellence, where first-class tuition and facilities were on offer.

'There was going to be a residential side to the sports precinct so that people could travel here for sporting holidays and indulge themselves in their passion,' Harvey said. Even day visitors would have private rooms so they could fully relax and entertain their friends. It was to be a complete package which could be promoted widely.

A number of investors banded together, combining their modest equity and borrowing capacity. Plans were duly prepared and lodged with council. 'Everyone was on side,' said Harvey. 'The council wanted the project, local sports professionals were keen to get involved, advertisers were discussing sponsorship deals and tournaments at the facility, tourism organisations loved the scheme and offered support.

'But local community opposition was unexpected—and fierce. There was no logical reason for people to get so upset, particularly as there was going to be a sizeable buffer zone between the centre and the nearest houses. The fuss and clamour went on and on. We tried to sort it out but it became clear that no form of compromise would satisfy the objectors. In the end I pulled the plug on the project—even though council looked like issuing consent—as I did not want to live with ongoing bad press and publicity in my local community.'

It was an upsetting decision to have to make. Harvey had believed totally in the project. He knew he had council support for it. He had already invested a sizeable amount of money and, perhaps more significantly, time. Was it all for nothing?

Harvey had learnt many things from this, the 'one that got away'. He understood the meaning of the classic sports saying, 'it ain't over till it's over' (he had thought the project was in the bag when council came out strongly on side and the commercial endorsements were being discussed); he had seen just how unpredictable community objections could be—and just how much anger could be expressed towards the investors (he thought he was doing a *good* thing for the community and he would be appreciated for it).

Perhaps most interesting of all, however, was this observation: 'You get so close to a project,' said Harvey, 'that you ignore other possibilities. You narrow your focus until all you see is this one thing and you invest all your time and energy into it, to try and make the pieces fit. But you don't need to pressure yourself, to rush to catch the opportunity. Good investments are like buses . . . there's another one coming in five minutes' time.'

And that's precisely what Harvey did. He dusted himself off from the bad experience, found another investment opportunity and promptly made more money than he would have secured from his share of the sports centre. 'The next bus turned out to be a faster ride,' he said.

Property investment and transformation—even if the project involves nothing more than enclosing a strata unit balcony, adding a granny flat in the backyard or pushing through a doorway into the garden—are absorbing processes. They eat up our time and narrow our focus to the tasks immediately at hand. At best this process can also be fun and personally rewarding. But it is always just one of many ways of making some money and providing for our future.

Wise investors act counter to the prevailing cycle. They buy when prices are low and no one else is interested in that type of investment, and they sell when prices are high and that investment is in demand. We *know* that. But they're called 'wise' investors precisely because most of us smart investors don't act in this way. We're not dumb . . . but we find it hard to go against the flow. We stubbornly refuse to believe that a boom is over or that a financial corner has been reached. There is a feeling of safety if we stay with the pack and follow the current formula.

We strain and stretch our resources, but are we really getting ahead? Ask yourself this: did your home price go up in the last residential property boom? So what. The next house you want has slipped further out of your reach. Arguably, if you want to stay in the same part of town but upgrade, you've gone backwards financially.

Property transformation is our opportunity to 'make the jump to light speed' (as they say in literature). The multiplier effect of our effort and risk is magnified and can deliver a real financial lift to our financial situation. Or, if poorly executed, it can send us broke.

But there's more to the equation. Anyone can buy a stock which is rising in price or get a little property investment happening when interest rates are low. But it is a thing of beauty to take a property and develop its potential. This is where our personal creativity and financial acumen intersect. The process throws up a series of potent challenges which will try our intelligence, our diplomacy skills and our physical and emotional strength to the very limit. The potential rewards are measured in more than mere money, and we may fall on our face. Many of us simply have an urge to do it.

Property transformation is the athletics carnival of property investing. Are you ready to give it a run?

Resources, information and contacts

Land titles offices

This is the place to go to connect with information about land titles, registration, title conversion and to search property registers.

ACT: Land Titles, phone (02) 6207 0491, www.rgo.act.gov.au
NSW: Land and Property Information, phone (02) 9228 6666, www.lpi.nsw.gov.au
NT: Land Titles Office, phone (08) 8999 7743, www.nt.gov.au
Queensland: Department of Natural Resources and Mines, phone (07) 3405 6900, www.nrm.qld.gov.au/property/titles
SA: Lands Services, phone (08) 8226 3983, www.landservices.sa.gov.au
Tasmania: Land Services, phone (03) 6233 3506, www.dpiwe.tas.gov.au
Victoria: Title Registration Services, phone (03) 8636 2010, www.land.vic.gov.au
WA: Department of Lands Administration, phone (08) 9273 7373, www.dola.wa.gov.au

Industry associations

The Real Estate Institute

There is a national office and a separate office for each state and territory.

Real Estate Institute of the ACT: www.reiact.com.au
Real Estate Institute of New South Wales: www.reinsw.net.au
Real Estate Institute of Northern Territory Inc.:
www.reint.predelegation.com
Real Estate Institute of Queensland: www.reiq.com.au
Real Estate Institute of South Australia: www.reisa.com.au
Real Estate Institute of Tasmania: www.reit.com.au
Real Estate Institute of Victoria: www.reiv.com.au
Real Estate Institute of Western Australia: www.reiwa.com.au
The Property Council of Australia: www.propertyoz.com.au

Architects

The Royal Australian Institute of Architects is the principal industry association: www.architecture.com.au

For building inspection reports carried out by an architect, contact an architect direct or for a referral go to Archicentre at www.archicentre.com.au, phone 1300 134 513. Archicentre is the Building Advisory Service of the Royal Australian Institute of Architects. It is the largest supplier of design and pre-purchase home inspections in Australia. Its other services include running seminars, an architect's advice line, renovation reports, advice on building contracts and advice on dealing with councils.

Note that there is also the Association Consulting Architects Australia which is the employers' organisation for Architects in Australia, www.archioz.com.au

Surveyors

Surveyors have had a number of professional organisations promoting their interests. For referral to a surveyor, try phoning (02) 6282 2623 or go to www.surveying.org.au which is the site of the Association of Consulting Surveyors Australia (ACSA). The address is National Surveyors House, 27–29 Napier Close, Deakin, ACT, 2600.

Consulting engineers

The Association of Consulting Engineers Australia will help you find the engineer you need. At its website you can search mostly on issues of application to engineers, such as indemnity insurance: www.acea.aust.com

Registered property valuers

For a referral to a valuer or to find out about their code of conduct, contact the Australian Property Institute. There are state bodies but the national secretariat is at 6 Campion Street, Deakin, ACT, 2600, phone (02) 6282 2411. The national website is www.property institute.com.au

Finance

Contact the Financial Planning Association of Australia, phone 1800 337 301, or in Melbourne (03) 9627 5200, or for referral to a financial planner, phone 1800 626 393, www.fpa.asn.au

Tenancy information

Contact the Tenancy Information Centre of Australia, www.tica.com.au—a site very much for landlords.

Law societies

Do you need to find a solicitor? The local lawyers' society or institute will direct you:

ACT: The Law Society of the ACT, phone (02) 6247 5700, www.lawsocact.asn.au

NSW: Law Society of NSW, phone (02) 9926 0333, www.lawsocnsw.asn.au

NT: The Law Society of the Northern Territory, phone (08) 8981 5104, www.lawsocnt.asn.au
Qld: Queensland Law Society, phone (07) 3842 5888, www.qls.com.au
SA: Law Society of South Australia, phone (08) 8229 0222, www.lssa.asn.au
Tas: The Law Society of Tasmania, phone (03) 6234 4133, www.taslawsociety.asn.au
Vic: Law Institute of Victoria, phone (03) 9607 9311, www.liv.asn.au
WA: The Law Society of Western Australia, phone (08) 9322 7877, www.lawsocietywa.asn.au

Industry complaints handling schemes

Australian Banking Industry Ombudsman

The Ombudsman handles disputes involving member banks and can make an award in the consumer's favour up to a maximum of $150 000. There is no charge for this service. Phone 1300 780 808, www.abio.org.au

Credit unions and building societies

Complaints and disputes are handled by more than one potential agency. You may have to contact a couple of agencies before you find the right one for your particular financial institution.

The Financial Co-operative Dispute Resolution Scheme (FCDRS) deals with complaints from consumers about credit unions and building societies which are members of the scheme—issues such as ATM, eftpos and credit card disputes. Phone 1300 139 220, www.fcdrs.org.au. This scheme does not replace an earlier dispute resolution scheme for complaints involving credit unions which are members of the Credit Union Dispute Resolution Centre (CUDRC). Disputes with participating credit unions (which abide by a code of practice) are handled without charge to credit union members. The Centre has jurisdiction to handle a complaint concerning up to $100 000. A decision of the Centre is binding on the credit union but not on the customer. Phone 1300 780 808, www.cudrc.com.au

Building societies do not have their own dispute resolution scheme, but have officers trained to handle complaints. Contact the head office of the society or go to the Australian Association of Permanent Building Societies for information on what to do. Phone (02) 6281 1588, www.aapbs.com.au

Financial Industry Complaints Service Limited

This scheme handles disputes involving financial advice provided by a member of the Financial Planning Association. There is no charge for the service. An award in the consumer's favour can be made up to a maximum of $6000 per month for income protection insurance, $250 000 for life insurance and $100 000 for funds management, stock broking, investment and financial advice. Phone 1300 780 808, www.fics.asn.au

Insurance Enquiries and Complaints Ltd

This scheme primarily handles complaints involving motor vehicle property damage and your insurance company, but also provides free advice about general insurance: property, contents, landlord's policies and more (but not life insurance matters). The services are free of charge. Phone 1300 780 808, www.iecltd.com.au

The Insurance Brokers Disputes Limited

This service handles disputes with insurance brokers. It is free and can handle complaints worth up to $50 000 for general and life insurance. Phone 1800 064 169, www.hiba.com.au

Mortgage Industry Association of Australia

This is the industry body for non-bank mortgage providers, brokers and mortgage managers. There is a code of practice—check the website. Phone (02) 9967 2889, www.miaa.com.au

Mortgage Industry Ombudsman

The Mortgage Industry Association of Australasia (MIAA) established an ombudsman scheme in May 2000. It handles customer complaints about its members, provided the customer has already attempted to resolve the dispute directly with the member but is not satisfied with the outcome. Members of the MIAA agree to abide by a code of practice, part of which includes an obligation to empower the Mortgage Industry Ombudsman to investigate, negotiate and ultimately make a decision on a customer's complaint. A decision of the Ombudsman is binding on the Association member. An award can be made in favour of the customer up to a maximum of $100 000. The process is free of charge to the customer. Phone 1800 138 422 or, in Sydney, (02) 9267 1000, www.acdcltd.com.au

Property reports and marketing

Many real estate agents have their own individual websites. Contact them for the address. Here is a selection of more general property sites.

Domain

A Fairfax publications site, www.domain.com.au, Domain is a good place to check real estate advertisements from the Fairfax publications around Australia. You can get a suburb snapshot, ask to be electronically alerted when a type of property is advertised and can save particular property ads to your own short list file. A mortgage comparison tool is also available.

Australian Property Monitors

This site sells property reports—you can select by postcode, suburb or even by street name. Auction results and a free email newsletter can keep you up to date: www.homepriceguide.com.au or www.apm.com.au

HomePath

HomePath is an information site which is a subsidiary of the Commonwealth Bank. Free registration brings you information on aspects of buying, selling and investing in property, including calculators, some price data and a personalised property alert function: www.homepath.com.au

Property

Here is a general website of interest (searching, getting an agent, finance): www.property.com.au

PropertyWeb

Although the focus here is largely on commercial and industrial property, there is still good information for those looking for homes or residential investments. Auction clearance rates and volumes (in price brackets) are a highlight feature. An interesting range of articles can be found here too: www.propertyweb.com.au

Realestate property searching

www.realestate.com.au

Residex

Here you can get hold of price information and reports for Queensland and New South Wales for a fee. Performance predictions are a feature. Residex links to www.findmeahome.com.au, where you can search for a property and mortgage: www.residex.com.au

Your finances

Interest rates

Here are some sites where you can find current interest rates for loans from a wide range of financial institutions:

Cannex	www.cannex.com.au
Interestrate	www.interestrate.com.au
Ninemsn	www.money.ninemsn.com.au
Yahoo	www.yahoo.com.au
eChoice	www.echoice.com.au

Financial product comparison

If you want some guidance and assistance with comparing various financial products (banking, loans, deposits, managed funds), go to these websites:

Cannex	www.cannex.com.au
Infochoice	www.infochoice.com.au
Personal Investor	www.personalinvestor.com.au
Your Mortgage	www.yourmortgage.com.au

Financial planning

The following websites are useful for information on integrating your financial and investment projects:

Ninemsn: www.money.ninemsn.com.au
Moneymanager: www.moneymanager.com.au, part of the f2 network
ING Financialpassages: www.ing.com.au
AMP has a fine personal finance site: www.amp.com.au
InvestorWeb: www.investorweb.com.au—good for property trusts
Financial Planning Association: Here you'll find information on licensed financial planners and assistance via an online referral service: www.fpa.asn.au

Magazines

Four of my favourite financial information sites are prepared by magazine publishers. They have useful calculators and carry helpful articles in a magazine style:

***Australian Property Investor* magazine**	www.apimagazine.com.au
Personal Investor	www.personalinvestor.com.au
CHOICE Money and Rights	www.choice.com.au
Your Mortgage	www.yourmortgage.com.au

Online mortgage providers and brokers

There are many of these now. Don't know which loan is right for you? Online mortgage finders will help you. Here is a selection to get you started.

www.echoice.com.au
www.wizard.com.au
www.homeloansnow.com.au
www.isay.com.au
www.mortgagechoice.com.au
www.mortgagehouse.com.au
www.peachhomeloans.com.au
www.yeshomeloans.com.au

Financial institutions

Looking for the website for a particular bank or other lender? Try inserting the name of the institution, as in these examples:

www.anz.com.au
www.aussiehomeloans.com.au
www.commbank.com.au (Commonwealth Bank)
www.imb.com.au
www.national.com.au (National Australia Bank)
www.westpac.com.au
www.wizard.com.au

Credit

Your credit record

At Baycorp Advantage, you can check your credit record for a fee, and see what it says about you. Go to www.mycreditfile.com.au

Consumer Credit Code

Find out about a lender's obligations under the Credit Code, including the mandatory use of a comparison rate in advertising, at www.creditcode.gov.au

Taxation

Stamp duty

For inquiries and information, call your state or territory revenue office or go to its website:

ACT: Phone (02) 6207 0028, www.revenue.act.gov.au
NSW: Phone (02) 9685 2122 or 1300 139 814, www.osr.nsw.gov.au
NT: Phone (08) 8999 7949, www.nt.gov.au/ntt/revenue
Qld: Phone 1300 300 734, www.osr.qld.gov.au
SA: Phone (08) 8204 9870, www.revenuesa.sa.gov.au
Tas: Phone (03) 6233 3566, www.treasury.tas.gov.au
Vic: Phone 13 21 61, www.sro.vic.gov.au
WA: Phone (08) 9222 8866, www.dft.wa.gov.au

Land tax

For inquiries and information, call your state or territory revenue/land tax office, or go to its website:

ACT: Phone (02) 6207 0049, www.revenue.act.gov.au
NSW: Phone (02) 9685 2188 or 1300 139 816,
www.osr.nsw.gov.au
NT: www.nt.gov.au/ntt/revenue
Qld: Phone (07) 3227 6044 or 1300 301 547, www.osr.qld.gov.au
SA: Phone (08) 8204 9870, www.revenuesa.sa.gov.au/taxes
Tas: Phone (03) 6233 3566, www.treasury.tas.gov.au
Vic: Phone 13 21 61, www.sro.vic.gov.au
WA: Phone (08) 9222 8866, www.dft.wa.gov.au

Income tax

Contact the Australian Taxation Office. The phone line for personal tax inquiries is 13 28 61, www.ato.gov.au

Goods and Services Tax (GST)

Contact the Australian Taxation Office or head to its website at www.ato.gov.au. Phone the Business Infoline on 13 28 66 or obtain *A Fax from Tax* on 13 28 60.

Consumer protection agencies and associations

Australian Competition and Consumer Commission

This independent statutory authority of the Commonwealth government administers the Trade Practices Act, Prices Surveillance Act and many other pieces of legislation. Phone 1300 302 502, www.accc.gov.au

Australian Securities and Investments Commission (ASIC)

Information phone line 1300 300 630, www.asic.gov.au and see ASIC's consumer and investor website, called fido, at www.fido.asic.gov.au

Commonwealth Ombudsman

The Ombudsman investigates complaints about Commonwealth government departments, agencies and officers: phone 1300 362 072, www.comb.gov.au

Consumers Online

This is the Commonwealth Government's consumer protection site: www.consumersonline.gov.au

Department of the Treasury, Consumer Affairs Division

This division looks after product safety recalls and some elements of consumer protection education and policy: www.treasury/gov.au

State and territory consumer affairs

Australian Capital Territory Office of Fair Trading, phone (02) 6207 0400, www.fairtrading.act.gov.au

New South Wales Department of Fair Trading, phone 13 32 20, www.fairtrading.nsw.gov.au

Northern Territory Department of Justice—Consumer and Business Affairs, phone (08) 8999 1999, www.caba.nt.gov.au

Queensland Office of Fair Trading, phone (07) 3246 1500, www.fairtrading.qld.gov.au

South Australian Office of Consumer and Business Affairs, phone (08) 8152 0732, www.ocba.sa.gov.au

Tasmanian Office of Consumer Affairs and Fair Trading, phone (03) 6233 7667, www.justice.tas.gov.au/ca

Consumer Affairs Victoria, phone (03) 9627 6000, www.consumer.vic.gov.au

Department of Consumer and Employment Protection—Consumer Protection Division, phone (08) 9244 1299, www.docep.wa.gov.au

The Australian Consumers' Association (ACA)

This independent, non-party-political consumer organisation pubishes *CHOICE* magazine and is the lobbying organisation for consumer protection and policy development. Phone (02) 9577 3333, www.choice.com.au

Builder licensing authorities and associations

ACT: ACT Planning and Licensing Authority (ACTPLA), builders' licensing section, phone (02) 6207 1926, www.actpla.act.gov.au

NSW: Department of Fair Trading, phone 13 32 20 or (02) 9895 0111, www.fairtrading.nsw.gov.au

NT: Department of Infrastructure, Planning and Environment—Building Advisory Services, phone (08) 8999 8911, www.ipe.nt.gov.au. At the time of writing there is no licensing scheme, but it is anticipated a scheme will be introduced in 2004.

Qld: The Queensland Building Services Authority (BSA), phone (07) 3225 2800, www.bsa.qld.gov.au

SA: Office of Consumer and Business Affairs, Builders Licensing, phone (08) 8204 9644, www.ocba.sa.gov.au

Tas: Department of Infrastructure, Energy & Resources. It is not a general licensing system, but a scheme for accreditation of the 'principal builder' on the site. Phone 1300 135 513, www.wst.tas.gov.au/building

Vic: Building Commission Victoria, phone (03) 9285 6400, www.buildingcommission.com.au

WA: Builders Registration Board, phone (08) 9476 1200, www.brb.org.au

Housing Industry Association Ltd

This is a national association (with state branches) for the building trades. Consumer line 1902 973 555, www.buildingonline.com.au

Master Builders Australia

The major Australian association for the building and construction industry. There are state and national organisations. Phone (02) 6249 1433, www.masterbuilders.com.au

Glossary

AAPR this stands for Average Annualised Percentage Rate and is one of several methods of comparing one loan deal with another by incorporating the interest rate, any lower introductory rate, fees and charges. The aim is to quantify the true cost of the loan over a period of time. Other terms in use include 'effective rate' and 'comparison rate'. Each method will have its own way of making the comparison, so one set of figures might not actually provide a fair comparison with another if they were worked out under different methods. See *CCRL.*

allotment a block of land subdivided out of a larger section.

amenity the pleasantness of a place. The amenity of a street, for example, will be an amalgam of such features as the type and number of trees and bushes, the air quality, wide boulevard or narrow lane, noise and traffic.

auction the public sale of property to the highest bidder on the fall of the hammer.

bank cheque a cheque issued by the bank on its account.

body corporate the council or committee comprising unit owners which controls a strata/unit development, including the buildings and common property.

bond a security for money lent by an investor to a company, the government or a government agency—e.g. government (treasury) bonds. The money is lent for a fixed term at a fixed interest rate.

bridging finance a short-term loan to help a person complete the purchase of a property before they have sold their existing property.

capital accumulated wealth—a lump sum of money or other assets after deducting debt.

Capital Gains Tax (CGT) this is a Commonwealth tax payable on the increase, if any, in the value of a listed asset (such as shares or property) between the time it was purchased or acquired and the time when it is sold or disposed of. The family home is generally exempt from CGT. CGT only applies to assets purchased or acquired after 19 September 1985.

capped loan a loan where the interest rate has an upper limit.

caveat a warning notice placed on the legal title to a property by someone other than the registered owner, claiming an interest in the property. While the caveat is present, it will prevent the sale of the property and may make it difficult to borrow money using the property as security for the loan.

CCRL This is the Compulsory Comparison Rate prescribed by the Compulsory Comparison Rate Legislation (CCRL) which took effect nationally from 1 July 2003 under the Consumer Credit Code. This law requires financial institutions to specify the 'comparison rate' in their fixed-term consumer credit advertising and promotions (that is, it excludes 'indefinite' credit products such as credit cards and line-of-credit loans). The comparison rate is based on the interest rate of the loan (including any cheaper rate during the initial period) plus fees and charges, calculating an all-up cost of the loan over a set period. The scheme will be reviewed in 2006. The previous comparative scheme was called AAPR: see *AAPR* and Chapter 10.

community title this is the name given, in some states, to a form of property ownership designed for a mixture of uses, from residential to commercial and industrial, within the one development. It may be used to create a resort, for example—bringing together villas, apartments, shops, a golf course, marina and tennis court with roads and other infrastructure.

company title this is an older form of title, generally pre-dating strata title, which uses a company structure to subdivide and own a property, creating separate units. Each property owner actually owns a share or number of shares in the company. Company title is now usually found only in old apartment blocks, some of which are run down and others highly prized and exclusive. Company title properties often are more difficult to sell than a strata/unit title property, and this is reflected in generally lower prices. This situation arises because there may be restrictive conditions in the company documents which set out the agreement between the shareholders. For example, it may be necessary to obtain the consent of the other owners to a prospective purchaser of 'your' unit.

Consumer Price Index (CPI) a measure of the cost of living.

contract of sale the legal document setting out the terms and conditions for the sale and purchase of property.

conveyancing the process whereby ownership of a property lawfully passes to another. It generally involves checking that the vendor has full and proper legal title to the property, free of any encumbrance or hindrance. People usually engage a solicitor or licensed conveyancer to undertake this task, although there is nothing to stop a person performing their own conveyancing. However, a professional will carry indemnity insurance for the consequences of mistakes.

covenant a restriction on the legal title to property that either benefits or burdens the land (e.g. to specify what building materials or fencing can and cannot be used).

debenture this is a form of security for a debt—where the investor lends money to a bank, finance company or the like, wishing to raise capital; the investor receives a fixed interest rate on this loan.

default to break the terms of your mortgage contract with your lender. For example, to miss the due date for a repayment, or to fail to keep the mortgaged property insured.

deposit it is an almost universal requirement, under contracts for the sale and purchase of property, to require the purchaser to pay part of the sale price to the vendor at the time of entering into the contract, with the balance of funds to follow after a period of investigation of the property's legal title. The deposit is this first sum of money. Generally the contract for land will call for a 10 per cent deposit. The deposit can be lost to the vendor if the purchaser fails to complete the contract within the terms of the contract.

deposit bond when buying a property which is not yet completed—such as 'off the plan'—a purchaser can avoid having to pay the usual 10 per cent deposit on exchange of contracts. Certain financial institutions will pay the deposit for you and charge you a fee ranging from around half a per cent to almost 2 per cent of the full purchase price of the property. The actual amount varies according to the time period until completion of the building and the amount you want to borrow (the shorter the term and the smaller the amount mean a lower fee). This fee is not credited against the deposit, which you must pay at settlement or when the bond term expires.

development application (DA) an application to the local council seeking approval to develop a property. This might involve renovation, demolition, construction, subdivision or change of use (e.g. from residential to commercial).

discretionary trust a legal structure for owning property (and/or other assets). The trustee is in control, determining which beneficiaries receive income and in what amounts. It is a structure used for tax planning and estate planning purposes.

drawdown to call loan monies from your lender/mortgagee and apply them to your purpose—for example, to pay for the purchase of your property or to pay out an earlier loan. In some situations, such as when building or renovating a property, there may be more than one drawdown of funds over a period of time.

easement a right to do something—such as walk or drive—over the land of another; generally the owner of the encumbered (burdened) land cannot build over the site of the easement or block the passage.

encumbrance a burden on a property giving legally enforceable rights to someone who is not the owner of the property—for example, a right of access, a driveway, a water course, a covenant (e.g. restricting the use of certain building materials) or a mortgage. The existence of the encumbrance will be revealed by a search of the title documents or certificate of title for the property. It is part of the role of a conveyancer to search for encumbrances and report to their client (purchaser, mortgagee) on their meaning and impact.

equity the net capital value of an asset free of all loans and debts. For example, if you own a property valued at $100 000 and it is subject to a mortgage of $38 000, your equity in the property is $62 000. This is not to be confused with *equities*.

equity loan a loan secured against the equity in a property.

establishment fee application fee for a loan.

exchange counterparts of the contract of sale for property are signed separately by the vendor and the purchaser. The contract is made, or comes into existence, when those signed counterparts are swapped, so that the vendor ends up with a copy of the contract signed by the purchaser and vice versa. The swapping is called 'exchange' of contracts. It is the moment when the contract comes into existence and from which any time limits specified in the contract start to run.

fee simple a legal interest in property or estate capable of being inherited without limitation. It is the highest form of ownership.

financial institution an organisation or company which deals in financial services, such as taking deposits and making loans. Examples include banks, building societies, credit unions and finance companies.

fixed rate a mortgage is said to be 'fixed rate' when the interest rate will not vary during the term of the loan. It will remain unchanged even though the cash rate rises or falls.

forfeit this means to take something from another. In the context of conveyancing, it generally means the purchaser has breached an important part of the contract and the vendor takes (forfeits) the purchaser's deposit money.

freehold ownership of property in *fee simple*.

GST abbreviation for Goods and Services Tax—a consumption tax at the rate of 10 per cent on most goods and services. The tax was introduced on 1 July 2000. Note that residential rent is exempt from GST.

guarantee a contractual promise to do something (e.g. to pay back a loan).

guarantor a person or company which gives a guarantee; this is generally given for the benefit of another. For example, a parent might guarantee the fulfilment of the obligations under a loan contract entered into by his or her child.

inclusions objects included in the sale/purchase of property, such as carpets, blinds, curtains, light fittings, TV antenna, clothes line and so on.

interest money paid by a borrower in return for the use of money lent by another, or money paid for not requiring a debt or loan to be repaid.

inventory a schedule of items included in the sale/purchase which are not attached to the property or fitted. For example, beds, cupboards, chairs, tables, rugs, mirrors.

joint tenants a legal mode of ownership of property by more than one person. Joint tenants own the whole of the property in equal shares. When one joint tenant dies, their share goes to the remaining joint tenants equally. See *tenancy in common*.

land tax a state/territory government tax on property ownership by value.

lease a legal agreement—not always in writing—by which the owner gives exclusive possession of a property to another, generally in consideration of the payment of rent.

lenders' mortgage insurance see *mortgage insurance.*

lessee tenant.

lessor landlord.

lot see *allotment.*

managing agent this is a person appointed by the owner of a rental property to manage that property. Tasks would generally include finding tenants, collecting rent, arranging quotes for maintenance and repairs, lodging bonds with relevant state authorities, preparing and issuing all notices to tenants required by law or lease and handling disputes with tenants, including appearing before tenancy tribunals. Where a body corporate passes some of its functions to a professional manager, that person might also be referred to as a managing agent.

margin loan a loan generally for the purpose of buying shares or units in managed funds.

margin scheme a transitional arrangement for calculation of GST on property which was owned prior to 1 July 2000 and developed or sold after that date. The calculation allows for the fact that part of the value of the property pre-dated the introduction of the tax. The result is that the GST rate is applied against a lower figure for the value of the property.

mortgage this is the name given to a loan which is secured against real estate—for example, the bank loan used to enable a person to buy a property or to raise money for other purposes, even if these have nothing to do with the property itself (such as a business loan or to pay for a holiday or support a line of credit). The mortgage contract and associated legislation permit the mortgagee to sell the security if the loan is in default.

mortgage insurance this is insurance to cover the situation where the borrower (mortgagor) defaults in payments to the lender (mortgagee) required by the mortgage and there is a shortfall when the property is sold. The premium is paid by the borrower, usually as a one-off payment at the commencement of the loan. It is not to be confused with income protection insurance, which replaces lost income where a person suffers illness or injury and is unable to work as before, or mortgage protection insurance (which covers loan repayments). It is now more commonly called lenders' mortgage insurance (LMI).

mortgagee the name given to the lender where the loan is secured against a property. The mortgagee may be the bank, finance company or even a family member.

mortgagor the name given to the borrower (and owner of the property) where a loan is secured against that property.

negative gearing a property used for investment is negatively geared when the net rent income, after deduction of operating expenses, is less than the interest paid on the borrowings (mortgage) used to purchase the property. This lowers the overall assessable income of the investor for taxation purposes.

notice to complete the contract for sale of property includes a provision for a party to the contract to issue a notice calling on a party in default to fulfil its obligations—for example, calling on the purchaser to pay the balance of the sale price and complete the contract. It will specify what will happen if the other party does not meet its contractual obligations by the notice deadline (for example, the contract will be terminated and any deposit monies will be forfeited).

off the plan selling or purchasing a unit or other lot in a development before construction is complete, after inspecting the architectural drawings and building plans.

old system title this is the original form of legal title (ownership) in Australia—it has largely been replaced by Torrens title. Ownership of old system title property relies on being able to prove an unbroken chain of title leading up to the vendor. The chain of title consists of the documents by which the property has been conveyed (sold), mortgaged and otherwise encumbered over the years, going back to what is called a 'good root of title'. State legislation covers many aspects of the operation of old system title.

option in the context of property, it is a legally enforceable right to buy a property before the expiry of a deadline and at a predetermined price. A fee will generally be paid for this privilege; the fee might be credited against the eventual purchase price for the property if the option is 'exercised', but this is not always the case.

outgoings these are expenses associated with owning and running the investment property from day to day. They include rates, gardening, managing agent's fees, insurances, strata/unit levies and maintenance.

principal the amount borrowed.

private sale sale of property by the owner, with or without a real estate agent being involved.

private treaty private sale of property (as opposed to the public sale of property at auction).

property syndicate a group of investors who put their money together to jointly buy one or more properties; a syndicate usually has a fixed term of five to ten years, after which the assets are sold and the net proceeds distributed; there are restrictions on getting your money out earlier.

provisional tax in the past, those who earned income from self-employment or investments (such as property) may have been required to pay income tax in advance in addition to normal income tax which was paid over the course of the previous tax year. This 'provisional tax' was then credited against actual tax payable when the next year's tax was assessed. A percentage 'uplift factor' was applied against this estimate of future tax, on the assumption that a person's income increased from year to year. From 1 July 2000 the system of provisional tax was replaced in Australia by the Pay As You Go scheme.

purchaser the buyer.

records financial records to do with your investment—receipts, invoices, rent statements, bank statements and so on—must be kept for five years from the date you lodge your tax return. For capital gains tax purposes, you must keep the records of your ownership and capital improvements for five years from the date you sell or otherwise dispose of the property.

redraw facility a benefit offered by some types of loan contract—including many, but not all, mortgages—which allows the borrower to take money back out of their loan account provided they have paid in advance of the minimum requirement of the loan contract. For example, if your mortgage requires you to make monthly loan repayments (principal and interest) of $1200 per month and in fact you accelerate your repayments by making monthly instalments of $1500 per month (or you make a lump sum deposit into the account to reduce the loan principal), you might be able to withdraw some of the excess if your loan contract allows 'redraws'. These might be free of charge or, particularly with 'no frills' mortgages, could cost tens of dollars each time. It is a very positive feature to look for in a home loan.

refurbish to decorate or fix up a property into good order. This might include painting, floor coverings, fixtures and fittings.

rent the money a property owner receives from the tenant in exchange for letting the tenant live in the property. It is commonly paid weekly or monthly. It is income for taxation purposes.

reserve the purchase price set by a vendor at auction below which the vendor will not sell the property.

Reserve Bank the Reserve Bank of Australia is the central bank of the Commonwealth of Australia. However, it operates independently of the government. Its task is to keep the economy healthy through maintaining desirable levels of inflation, growth and employment. One of its chief tools for achieving these aims is by establishing the cash rate—the basic building block for the interest rates used by financial institutions—and the availability of money to service the national economy.

stamp duty a state/territory government tax. Among many other situations, it is payable on the transfer of property or an interest in property. Generally, in conveyancing, it is payable by the purchaser, though this is not always the case.

strata title a form of Torrens title which allows a single property to be subdivided, including vertically. An example is a block of home units, where each unit has a separate title and can be sold and owned independently of the other units. There are privately owned lots and lots owned in common (e.g. staircases, gardens, pool, lift, the fabric of the building). In some places it is called 'unit title'.

subdivision to reconfigure the shape of an allotment or to divide an allotment of land into two or more allotments, each on a separate legal title. Each new allotment can be sold and purchased separately.

syndicate see *property syndicate*.

tenancy in common a legal system of ownership of property by more than one person. Tenants in common own the whole of a property in such proportions as the title deed indicates—the proportions do not have to be equal. This is useful when one part-owner contributes more than half the purchase price and both or all part-owners want to maintain ownership in their respective proportions. When a tenant in common dies, their share is passed according to the provisions of their will. It need not necessarily go to the surviving tenants in common. See *joint tenants*.

tenant the person or company renting property from a landlord.

Torrens title a form of legal ownership of real estate guaranteed by the state/territory government and based on a system of registration of interests and certificates of title.

transfer a document recording the change of ownership of real estate; it is designed to be placed on the public register at the Land Titles Office (or equivalent) and to change the details accordingly on the certificate of title.

trust see *discretionary trust*.

use local council zoning schemes specify a number of permitted and prohibited uses for properties in each zone. Sometimes these are listed and particularised and sometimes they are very general. Many of these uses require council consent. Similarly, to change the permitted and approved use of a property requires council consent.

valuation what the property is worth. A bank or financial institution will often require a valuation both to determine whether the property is in sound condition and to assess how much money it can safely lend using the property as security. Sometimes the valuation is a certificate from a licensed valuer, or simply a letter from an estate agent. In many cases, lenders will use the purchase price of a property as its valuation, particularly where that property was purchased through public auction and the amount of the loan being sought is a moderate proportion of that price.

variable rate a mortgage is said to have a 'variable rate' when the interest rate is free to change, up or down, in line with the terms of the mortgage. Usually any change will follow a move in the official cash rate.

vendor the seller.

yield the yield of an investment is the ratio of its income to its value.

Index

AAPR, 174, 205
ABN, 166–7
ageing population, 25, 35, 67
allotment, 205
amenity, 205
architect
  contacting, 194
  see also designer
Australian Business Number (ABN), 166–7
Australian Securities and Investments Commission (ASIC), 202

BA *see* building application
back-up strategies
  find a developer, 179
  investment partner, 184
  multiple approvals, 181–2
  rent it out, 178–9
  second financier, 181
body corporate
  committee, 205
  negotiating with, 30–1
  voting, 31–2
builder
  checking licences, 146, 147
  contract, 146, 148
  contract variations, 147, 148–50
  delays, 150–1
  industry associations, 204
  licensing authorities, 204
  remedies, 151–2
  termination, 152
  witholding payment, 152
building application, 112
Building Code of Australia, 125
building envelope, 90–2
building problems, 145–6
bushfires, 90, 96

capital gain, xi,
capital gains tax
  calculation, 163–4
  improvements to property, 164–5

cashflow, 63
change of use
  commercial, 82–5
charisma, 4
common property
  conversion to private use, 25–8
  improving common assets, 28
company title, 24–5, 206
comparison rate, 174–7
complaints
  industry bodies, 196–8
consumer protection
  agencies, 202–3
conveyancing, 207
costs
  project, 159
council
  contributions, 96, 157
council officers
  dealing with, 123–4
covenant, 95, 126
credit, 201

DA *see* development application
deposit, 207
deposit bond, 208
design brief, 137–41
designer
  architect, 131–2
  choice of, 130–1, 132, 133
  cost, 132
  cross-cultural, 141–3
  design brief, 137–41
  what can go wrong, 133–7
development
  application, 111
  consent, 111–12, 118
  consent authority, 111
  construction certificate, 112
  controls, 117, 124–5
  costs, 157
  multiple approvals, 181–4
  precedent, 124–5
  pre-lodgment meeting, 76
disclaimer, viii

easement, 95, 126, 208
education zoning, 81
encumbrances on title, 95, 126, 208
energy efficiency, 125
engineer
  contacts, 195
  report, 73
environmental concerns, 96
excavation, 61, 65
exchange of contracts, 209
expert witness, 121

finance
  long-term, 70
  mezzanine, 172–3
  strategies, 169–72
financial planning, 200
financial product comparison, 199
finish
  level of, 140
floorplan, 35, 37, 40, 65
floorspace ratio, 117
footprint, 46–7

Goods and Services Tax (GST)
  Australian Business Number
    (ABN), 166–7
  commercial tenancy, 82
  contacts, 202
  margin scheme, 167–9
  registering, 166–7
granny flat, 68

heritage, 76, 96–7
housing orientation, 42

income tax
  contacts, 202
  pre-payment of interest, 166
  witholding variation, 165–6
indemnity, 28
interest
  pre-payment, 166
interest rates
  AAPR, 174
  comparison rates, 174–7
  resources, 199

joint tenants, 210

kitchen, 43

lame duck properties, 39–40
land tax
  vacant land subdivision, 90
  websites, 202
land titles offices, 193
law societies, 195–6

maintenance, 32–4
managing agent, 210
margin scheme, 167–9, 211
marketing, 6, 47–52, 54–8
materials, 138–9
medium-density housing,
  demand, 67
  guidelines, 74–6
  sizing up a site, 77–8
  townhouses, 71–3
mezzanine finance, 172–3
mortgage
  eliminating, 68
  refinancing, xiii

negative gearing, 211

objections
  defensive strategies, 116–17
  handling them, 113–14,
    120–1
  making them, 115–16
  who gets notified?, 114
  written, 117
off the plan, 212
old system title, 212
overcapitalisation, 47–9, 54,
  72

parking, 83
partners, 9
  negating partnership, 17
  see also syndicates
permitted use
  boarding house, 81
  changing, 79ff, 80, 87
  childcare facility, 80
  education, 81
  principles, 85–6
  residential to commercial,
    82–3, 84–5

retirement housing 81–2
tourism, 81
privacy, 96
property
reports, 198–9

Real Estate Institute, 193–4
redraw, 213
refinancing, xiii
renovation
expenditure, 37
house strategies, 41–3
overcapitalisation, 47–9
rent
subdivision of vacant land, 89
returns
measuring as rent, 62–3
right of way, 126
roadworks, 89, 94

safety plan, 58–9
security, 29, 31, 35, 65
solicitors, 94
stamp duty
on mortgage, 161
on purchase/transfer, 160–1
websites, 201
strata title
body corporate, 30–1
buying off the plan, 212
common property conversion to private use, 25–8
development strategies, 19ff
opportunities, 35
voting, 31–2
streetscape, 75
subdivision
approval, 113
backyard, 69
battle-axe, 99–100
dormitory, 100
face-to-face, 101
off the grid, 101
pros and cons of land subdivision, 88–90
road or driveway?, 102–3
shape and access options, 99–104
sizing up a site, 105–6
terrace houses, 102
surveyor, 77, 94, 103, 194
syndicates,
contracts, 17–18
forming, 15–18
strategies, 16–17

technology
car spaces, 23–5, 33–4
tenancy in common, 214
terminology, 111–12
title
company, 24–5, 29–30
converting, 29-30
tourism zoning, 81
town planning consulant, 93-4, 119-23
transformation gain, xi, xii

utilities, 158

vacancy rates, xiv
valuable spaces, 20-1

valuer
  contacts, 195
  report, 175-6
views, 96, 125

water, 95, 106

yield, x, xi, 53

zoning, 79, 82-3, 92, 117

Printed in Dunstable, United Kingdom

91224060R00136